Social Dance

FROM

Dance A While

Jane A. Harris
Anne M. Pittman
Marlys S. Waller

ALLYN AND BACON BOSTON LONDON TORONTO SYDNEY TOKYO SINGAPORE

Vice president, social sciences: Sean W. Wakely
Publisher: Joseph E. Burns
Series editorial assistant: Sara Sherlock
Marketing manager: Patricia Fossi
Composition and prepress buyer: Linda Cox
Manufacturing buyer: Suzanne Lareau
Cover administrator: Jenny Hart
Cover designer: Suzanne Harbison
Editorial-production administrator: Mary Beth Finch
Editorial-prodution service: Shepherd, Inc.
Text designer: Seventeenth Street Studios

A Viacom Company
Needham Heights, Massachusetts 02194

Internet: www.abacon.com
America Online: keyword: College Online

Harris, Jane A.
Social dance : from Dance a while/Jane A. Harris, Anne M. Pittman, Marlys S. Waller.
p. cm.
Includes index.
ISBN 0-205-27477-3
1. Ballroom dancing– Study and teaching. I. Pittman, Anne. II. Waller, Marlys S. III. Title
GV1753.5.H37 1998
793.3'3–dc21 97–44375
CIP

Printed in the United States of America.

10 9 8 7 6 5 4 3 2 1 02 01 00 99 98 97

Contents

Foreword

My earliest experience with *Dance A While* came in 1964 when, as a graduate student, I purchased my first copy. In 1969, Anne Pittman hired me as an Instructor of Modern Dance at Arizona State University. There was absolutely no connection between the two events. Over the years I accumulated revised editions of the book and Anne became a source of inspiration as I developed appreciation for different dance forms and cultures. I do not teach in the areas of folk, social, and square; however, recently, I began serious study of ballroom dance and our ongoing dialogue has become more focused on that genre. Now with this new and separate edition, *Social Dance from Dance A While*, my connection with *Dance A While* is more direct and personal. I am delighted to have the honor of penning the foreword.

Change seems to be the only constant in our lives. As we hurtle to the end of this millennium, trends and practices in the arts and society shift so quickly we find ourselves desperately attempting to find a sure footing somewhere. Those of us in dance are truly fortunate because we maintain contact with our sanity and stabilize ourselves, literally and metaphorically, by keeping our two feet either on, or at least in the reassuring proximity of, firm ground.

We take some solace when confronted with so much chaos by reminding ourselves that if we are not happy with the way things are, we need only to wait a few minutes, and change will occur. We also know from studying the past that cycles of approximately every twenty and fifty years bring a nostalgic return to some flavor of a previous, and sometimes more comforting, time. Today's focus on the "retro" look in fasion and disco, parallels a resurgence of interest in ballroom, Latin, and social dancing in general. Discussions of ballroom as Dance Sport in the Olympics also points to the enormous expansion and appreciation of social and ballroom dance forms.

Dance A While, a seminal work in the field, has played a significant role in keeping social and folk dance forms alive and accessible. It is inevitable that it, too, go through multiple permutations and evolve into a new form. As we prepare to enter the next period in history, the decision to create a separate handbook for social dance seems timely and appropriate. Teachers and practitioners of social dance will find this handbook useful for one of the book's original purposes—to introduce beginning and intermediate dancers to the exciting world of social and ballroom dance. It brings us up-to-date on the latest styles, changes, and resources available. Teachers have the privilege of sharing with students the unique body knowledge and experience that comes only through dance participation. Many generations to come, happily, will be influenced by this, and subsequent editions, of this valuable resource.

Beth C. Lessard, Ph.D., Professor
Former Chairperson (1977–1994)
Department of Dance
Arizona State University

Preface

The deed is done! We have separated the social dance section out of *Dance A While* to meet the needs of teachers and students who are interested in only one form of dance. Readers will now have a smaller, more economical textbook covering the same material found in the 7th edition of *Dance A While* published in 1994. *Dance A While* will continue to carry all forms of dance as it has in past editions. This special edition of *Social Dance* has been written, in part, to economize on space thus on price. Teachers will find greater detail in dance background, teaching, and lesson planning in the main text. We sincerely hope that our old and new readers will find *Social Dance from Dance A While* an effective and efficient reference for teaching and learning these exciting ballroom favorites.

Anne M. Pittman
Marlys S. Waller

Acknowledgments

Over the forty-four years of publication it has been our custom to research and write a different section with each revision of *Dance A While.* The authors, therefore, have had a very close working knowledge of the materials in each dance form. *Social Dance from Dance A While* is a spin-off of materials found in the social dance section of the main text. We would like to express our great appreciation to our former co-author and colleague Jane A. Harris (Ericson) for her extensive work in developing the format and content of this section.

In addition to the materials from the main text we have been generously assisted by Kathy Du Bois of the University of Wisconsin, La Crosse, in updating the Country Western and Line dances. We are grateful to Kathy and Sue Lipscomb, who each contributed an original Country Western Line dance. And very special "kudos" to our longtime friend Henry "Buzz" Glass for two original line dances, a Tango and a Caribbean rhythm dance that add greatly to the diversity of the Line dance section. A "salute" to the reviewers who have helped move this project to fruition: Janice M. Bibik, University of Delaware; Lenna De Marco, Glendale Community College; Elizabeth Gibbons, East Stroudsberg University; and Joanne L. Lawrence, Weber State University.

Last but not least, a very special "thank you" to Marlys S. Waller for her many contributions and especially for attending classes at the Seattle Mountaineers to learn Zydeco! *Social Dance from Dance A While* benefits greatly from Marlys and Anne's grassroots research and the energy to apply it beyond forty-four years!

Social Dance

INTRODUCTION

Dance and music are not static forms. They mirror the culture in which they exist by reflecting the past, present, and any intercultural exchanges that have occurred. The everchanging human scene is absorbed and acted out in dance and music forms.

In the past, the Renaissance saw the royal courts of Europe vying with each other by staging elaborate costumed balls danced to the music of Beethoven, Brahms, and Strauss. In Colonial America, military balls and elaborate cotillions were popular. The hearty pioneers brought dance to the taverns and honky-tonks with their western migration. In more modern times, college proms and special festive occasions were the impetus for social dancing. Night clubs became the ballrooms for the dancing public. Clubs often specialized in a particular type of dance such as Country Western Swing of one variety or the other, Latin or simply an evening of ballroom favorites danced to the "big band" sound. Social dance has always been a viable part of the social life in America.

Phases of Social Dance

Since the 1900s, seven periods have marked the progress of Social Dance and each was stimulated or motivated by a new style of music. The *Foxtrot* had its beginnings in the early 1900s as a fast trotting step to a new jazz called "ragtime." Novelty dances like the Bunny Hug and the Grizzly Bear were widely popular during World War I. Next came Dixieland jazz and an athletic dance called the Charleston. Although a strenuous dance done to a syncopated beat, it found great favor among those sporting the "flapper style" of dress and look of the Roaring Twenties.

From the 1930s to the 1950s, big band music produced hundreds of tunes that have become classics. The *Lindy*, also called jitterbug and later Swing, made its appearance. Big band music changed the Foxtrot into a smooth dance with many variations. Even the waltz took on a new, more sophisticated look. The Big Apple, Shag, and Lambeth Walk were the main dance interest of the college crowd. The popularity of dancing to big band music increased the need for and the number of dance studios. The swinging and swaying of big band music also gave rise to large public ballrooms across the country. Although the Swing faded with the demise of the big bands, it returned in the 1980s and 1990s to be danced to a variety of rhythm styles of the period.

The *Tango* was a fad during the 1920s and has remained a ballroom favorite over the years, although at times overshadowed by interest in other

Latin dances. Stimulated by an influx of Latin music, the Cuban Rumba started a new trend toward Latin dances in the 1930s. The Brazilian Samba, Mambo, Cha Cha Cha, Calypso, Merengue, and later the Bossa Nova all enjoyed brief but exciting periods of popularity. The Tango, however, has endured as a ballroom favorite.

The beat and sound decibels produced by Rock music demanded a dance response that was to characterize the period during and after World War II. Rock and Roll was the music of such legends as Elvis Presley, the Beatles, Rolling Stones, and the Beach Boys. Dance movement became unencumbered by pattern or partner except as the dance action was performed facing and gyrating with another person. Dance bands and dance floor space became smaller. Disc jockeys and recorded music became the norm. Novelty or fad dances such as the Twist, Slop, Mashed Potato, Swim, Monkey, Pony, Bug, Hitch Hiker, Watusi, Hully Gully, and the Jerk enjoyed various degrees and length of popularity. Television and videos became the major vehicles for disseminating Rock and Roll music, dance, manners, and dress.

Country Western had its roots in the music and songs brought by European immigrants to the Appalachian Mountains in the Eastern United States. The mix of people from this region with a wider spectrum of people during World War II lead to an explosion of interest in the music and songs of these mountain people. Songs and music of the cowboys from Texas and the Southwest had generally become entrenched after the Civil War. These two music and dance forms coupled with the adaption of western cowboy dress became what is now known as Country Western. Country Western radio stations have long enjoyed popularity with a loyal listening public.

Swing, Disco Swing, and Country Swing are the basic patterns used in dancing to Country Western music. Line dancing has emerged to take its place alongside Country Western dance. Both enjoy a wide following and are danced to the same music at the same time. While couples dance in the line of direction around the dance floor, line dancers carry on in the center moving forward and back or sideways without interfering with the traditional flow of dancers around the perimeter.

From the inner cities comes Street dance. *Break dancing* and Hip Hop have roots in African American culture. Break dancing is an acrobatic form coming out of New York's south Bronx. Hip Hop has its roots in rap, but also embraces soul, funk, jazz, and dance hall reggae. The acompaning music is electronic funk with a machine-gun style chanting called rap.

■ *Vintage Dance*

Dances through the ages have cast their spell. They are a part of the common culture and a heritage to be borrowed, shared, and re-created. Thus, it is not surprising that there is, at present, considerable interest in reconstructing the ballroom dances of the 19th and early 20th centuries. Staging quadrilles, contras, waltzes, polkas, rags, and tangos provide a rich opportunity for research and re-creation in the areas of costuming, makeup, lighting, sound, and expanding dance skills.

It appears, therefore, that dance and the music that influenced it have come full circle. Big bands and partner or "touch" dancing have reappeared. Live bands playing a variety of rhythms such as Foxtrot, Swing, Latin, Rock, and Jazz are back in demand. Variety in music spawns variety in dance forms. America is dancing and dancing in style!

1

Teaching Social Dance

DEALING EFFECTIVELY WITH inherent variables such as class size, available space, length of unit, and materials to be taught is of prime importance to both the teaching and learning process. The following teaching techniques should be carefully utilized in relation to these variables.

Formations

The line, single line facing one direction or parallel lines with partner couples facing, is a highly effective formation to use in a social dance class. This formation allows students to see and hear the demonstration clearly. It also allows the teacher to face the class for explanations and turn his or her back to the class for demonstration purposes. When there are two teachers, each can work with his or her back to a line in the parallel line formation. In the single line, couples may be side by side. In the parallel line, couples are opposite. The line formations are especially essential when teaching beginning steps.

Walk-Through

The teacher should be clearly seen and heard while demonstrating and analyzing the action of a step. On cue, the class should then follow through several times. The walk-through tempo should begin slowly then gradually increase until it is up to the tempo of the music to be used. The step should be tried first to music without a partner then with a partner and music. A time "free of instructional direction" should be provided after the walk-through. During this time the teacher should circulate among the dancers giving individual assistance as needed.

The Cue

The whole principle of unison practice to develop rhythmic awareness is contingent upon the accuracy of a system of cueing. A signal, such as "ready and," serves to start the dancers in unison. It is important that the cues be given rhythmically! This helps the student to feel the timing. A variety of cues are used to help the student remember the foot pattern as well as the rhythm. For example:

4/4	1–2	3	4
Rhythm cue:	slow	quick	quick
Step cue:	step	side	close
Direction cue:	turn	side	close
Style cue:	down	up	up
Warning cue:	"get ready for the break"		
Foot cue:	right	left	right

A good technique is to change from one cue to the other as needed. Cueing is a "help" not a "crutch" and should be abandoned as soon as the students appear to be secure in their execution. Cueing at any stage in the learning process is best when done over a sound system that amplifies the voice.

Demonstration

The advantages of demonstration are (a) it hastens learning when students see what is to be learned, (b) it facilitates learning the style and flow of dance movement, and (c) teaching requires less talking, therefore, more practice is available. Demonstration is most helpful a the following times.

1. At the beginning of the lesson with partner and music to give a whole picture of the pattern. This is also a good motivational device.
2. When presenting a new step. Demonstrate the man's and woman's parts separately then the leads as students take partners.
3. Demonstrate to teach style, leads and partner relationships, and timing.
4. Occasionally demonstrate incorrect form followed by correct form.
5. Demonstrate for clarification.

Unison versus Free Practice

The walk-through for a new step should be done in unison responding to teaching cues. The whole motion of the group assists in the learning process and allows the teacher the opportunity to spot problems. Teacher directed unison practice should be abandoned as soon as a majority have learned the step. Free practice transposes the class into a "natural" situation, more akin to the way it is to be done as a leisure pursuit.

At every level of progress in the teaching and learning process, the student should be made aware of the importance of rhythm and the use of space when moving around the dance floor. Understanding rhythm means that the man can more creatively combine and lead a variety of dance patterns to any given piece of music. Understanding space means that the man can lead his partner around the dance floor in the traditional line of direction and at the same time employ steps and dance positions that allow him to steer his partner through and around other dancers without interrupting his or their movements.

Dance Lesson Preparation

Teacher preparation should begin with selecting the basic step to be taught. Next analyze the underlying rhythm and know where the accent is placed in the music. Study the style of the movement used in the step and practice with the music so that it can be accurately demonstrated. One teacher will need to know both the man's and the woman's part and be able to demonstrate them with a student from time to time. Two teachers demonstrating is a more ideal situation, but one well prepared teacher can lead a good student after a class walk through usually without out-of-class practice. In addition, the teacher should carefully analyze the position, leads, style, and teaching cues for both the man's and woman's parts and develop routines for practicing the step forward, backward, or in place.

Sample Lesson Plan

The daily lesson plan should include learning objective, music selection, background information about the dance, teaching progression, and evaluation. Objectives are the perceived outcomes of the lesson. Example: Dance the magic step in time with the music. Select several records with moderate tempo to provide sameness of beat, yet variety of sound for class practice. Most dances have backgrounds stemming from a country, region, type of music, or a personality. This is a typical and viable model for creating a good and effective lesson plan.

Teaching Progression

The teaching progression is the blueprint of the lesson and should be a supportive guide for the teacher and an effective road map for the students to achieve the objectives of the plan. The lesson should proceed from the known to the unknown. Begin the lesson with a warm-up and review, which means dancing and polishing something already learned. Follow with new material that should constitute the greater portion of the lesson. Then add free practice time and give individual assistance as needed. Throughout the lesson be alert to partner changes so that there is an ample exchange of opportunities for each student to dance with skilled and less skilled dancers. The evaluation* should guide the teacher to class needs and provide the students with some positive sense of their progress. The most important thing is to teach with enthusiasm and make each lesson a fun-filled occasion.

Technology Aids Teaching

Modern audio products such as the variable speed tape deck and CD player, wireless microphone systems and "Dick Tracy-like" wireless remote wrist-

*Refer to Dance A While, 7th edition, Chapter Two, "Effective Group Instruction," pp. 30, 31.

watch combine to free dance teachers from the stationary microphone and record player. The wireless microphone system consists of a light wire frame attached to the head and plugged into a belt pack transmitter thus giving the teacher complete mobility and easy vocal command during instruction. Depending on the manufacturer, the equipment has a range of 300 to 1000 plus feet and battery life of 15 to 18 hours. The wireless remote wristwatch makes it possible to control one CD and two tape decks. In addition, it starts and stops the music, adjusts the tempo, rewinds, moves fast forward, and can choose tracks on one or two CD decks.

STYLE OF SOCIAL DANCE

American Ballroom Dancing has borrowed steps and dances from many, many countries. Few of these are now done in the authentic style of any country. In most cases, it was the rhythmic quality that was fascinating, and not its meaning. Therefore, only a semblance of the original style remains in the Latin American dances done on our dance floors.

Particular consideration needs to be given to the importance of the individual as a person and the development of one's own style. Since all individuals are different, it is folly to try to get them all to perform exactly alike. The individual who likes to dance will work for the right feeling and take a pride in the way it looks. The dance will gradually reflect an easy confidence and become part of the individual's personality.

At the beginning, few students realized the importance of good basic posture and footwork to the beauty and style of any dance. An easy, upright, balanced posture and motion of the feet in line with the body will make the dancer look good regardless of how limited the knowledge of steps. Style means the specific way of moving in any one dance as influenced by rhythmic qualities of the music, cultural characteristics of a country, or the current style of the movement. Styles of dances change from time to time with the rising popularity of a new star, a new band sound, or a new promotional venture by the popular dance studios.

Footwork in Social Dance

Footwork is a term used to discuss the manner of using the feet in the performance of dance steps. With the exception of body posture, it has the most significant bearing on form and style. Far too often the placement of the feet and the action of the legs give a distorted appearance to the dance. The beauty, continuity, and balance of a figure may be lost entirely due to any comic and, at the same time, tragic caricature unintentionally given to the motion.

Some general principles are involved in the application of good footwork to good dance style.

1. The weight should be carried on the ball of the foot for easy balance, alert transfer of weight from step to step, and change of direction.
2. The feet should be pointing straight ahead. When moving from one step to another, they should reach straight forward or backward in the direction of the desired action and in line with or parallel to the partner's feet.
3. Any action will start with feet together. When moving, feet should pass as closely as possible. With a few exceptions, the feet should always come together before reaching in a new direction. This known as a follow-through with the feet, and it is used in the Foxtrot, Waltz, and Tango.
4. The feet are never dragged along the floor from one step to another, but are picked up and placed noiselessly in the new position. Occasionally, as in the Tango, the foot glides smoothly into place with the two reaching and without a scraping sound on the floor.
5. The legs should reach forward or backward from the hip. The action is initiated by stabilizing the trunk and swinging the leg freely.
6. The faster the rhythm, the shorter the step. The slower the rhythm, the more reaching the step.
7. Changes of direction are more readily in balance and under control if initiated when the feet are close together rather than when they are apart.
8. For the specific actions of reaching with one foot forward or backward, as in a corté or a hesitation step, the arch of the foot should be extended and the toe pointed.
9. Turning and pivoting figures are most effectively executed from a small base of support with the action of the man's and the woman's feet dovetailing nicely. This is possible when the action of the foot is a smooth turn on the ball of the foot with the body weight up, not pressing into the floor.
10. In accordance with the characteristic cultural style of a dance, the footwork will involve specific and stylized placement of the feet. This styling is described with each dance.

One-Step/Dance Walk

All smooth dances used to have a gliding motion with the ball of the foot. However, change in style now dictated a *dance walk* that is much like a regular walk when moving forward. It is a step forward on the heel of the foot, transferring the weight to the ball of the foot. This action is used by both man and woman when they are moving forward. The backward step is a long reach to the toe, transferring the weight to the ball of the foot.

In closed dance position, the man is reaching forward and the woman backward, simultaneously. There is a tendency for the man to step sideways so as not to step on the woman's foot, but he should step forward directly in line with her foot. The woman consequently must reach backward into her step not only to avoid being stepped on but to give him room for his step. Master dance teachers have been quoted as saying, "If the woman gets her toe stepped on, it is her own fault." This reemphasizes the point that the dance walk is a long reaching step and both man and woman must learn to reach out confidently. It is this reach that makes the style smooth and beautiful and provides contrast to other smaller steps. Taking all small steps gives the style a cramped, insecure feeling. The following points describe the mechanics of the forward dance walk.

1. The body sways forward from the ankles. The weight is on the ball of the foot.
2. The trunk is stabilized firmly. The leg swings forward from the hip joint. The reach results in a long step rather than a short, choppy step. An exaggerated knee bend will cause bobbing up and down.
3. The foot swings forward and the heel is placed on the floor first, followed by a transfer of weight to the ball of the foot. The feet never drag along the floor.
4. The legs are kept close together, with the feet passing closely together. The toes are facing straight ahead.
5. Man and woman dance on the same forward line. One should avoid letting one's feet straddle the partner's feet.

The backward dance walk is not an easy movement because one feels unstable moving backward. It should be practiced particularly by the woman since she will be moving backward a large part of the time.

1. The body weight is over the ball of the foot. One should take care not to lean forward or backward. The woman is pressing against the man's hand at her back.
2. The trunk is stabilized firmly. The leg swing backward from the hip joint with a long, smooth reach. Avoid unnecessary knee bend of the standing leg.
3. The foot is placed backward on the toe with weight transferring to the ball of the foot. The weight remains on the ball of the foot, the heel coming down only momentarily during the next step.
4. The legs and feet pass as closely as possible and in a straight line. One should avoid toeing out, heeling out, and swinging backward outside of the straight line.

DANCE POSITIONS

Successful performance with a dance partner depends on learning how to assume the dance positions* most often used in social dance: *closed position, open* or *conversation position, left parallel position, swing out* or *flirtation position, left parallel position, side car, shine, wrap, reverse open, and side-by-side position.* Dancers should learn how to assume the closed position as soon as they begin working with a partner. The results will lead to good balance, comfort, and confidence in leading and security in following. The closed position is the basic dance position. The others are adaptations of it.

■ *Closed Position*

Each factor in the analysis of the closed position is significant. It is not a mere formality. Those who are learning dance will tend to form better dance habits if they understand specifically how the position aids the dance rather than being left to manage as best they can.

1. **Partners should stand facing each other squarely with shoulders parallel.** When standing almost toe to toe, partners can maintain a comfortable distance and have freedom in leading and following. The body posture is in good alignment.
2. **The feet should be together and pointing straight ahead.** The weight is over the balls of the feet.
3. **The man's right arm** is placed around the woman so that his arm **gives her security and support. The right hand is placed in the center of the woman's back, just below the shoulder blades.** The fingers should be closed and the hand almost flat so that the man can lead with the fingers or the heel of the hand. The man's arm is extended away from his body with the elbow pointing slightly out to the right side. A majority of

*Refer to the glossary for descriptions of other positions.

leads are initiated by the man's shoulders, right arm, and hand.

4. **The woman's left arm rests gently but definitely in contact with the man's upper arm** and the hand should lie along the back of the man's shoulder as is comfortable. The woman's ability to follow is often determined by her response to the action of the man's arm.
5. **The woman should arch her back against the man's right hand and move with it.** All pressure leads for change of step will come from the man's right hand and she will feel them instantly.
6. **The woman's free hand is raised sideways and the man holds the woman's right hand in his left hand approximately between them at a level just above the woman's shoulder.** The man may let her fingers rest on his upturned palm, or he may grasp lightly with his thumb against her fingers and close his fingers around the back of her hand. He should not push with his hand.
7. **Both man and woman should look at each other or over the partner's right shoulder.**
8. **Resistance is essential.** A limp body or a limp hand is the surest indication of insecurity; a poor lead elicits a slow response. Dancers need to understand the difference between tension, which does not allow for easy moving along with one's partner, and relaxation, which cannot respond readily to change. An in-between state of body alertness–called resistance–is most desirable.

Some **common errors** in the use of closed position are the following:

1. Partner standing at an angle in a half-open position. This causes diagonal motion of the footwork and is uncomfortable.
2. Partner too far away.
3. Lack of support in the man's right arm.
4. Lack of contact of the woman's left arm.
5. Primary use of man's left hand to lead by a pushing or pumping action.
6. Lack of resistance by either man or woman.
7. Man's right hand too high on woman's back, pulling her off balance.
8. Woman's weight back on heels.
9. Man leaning forward from the waist off balance.
10. Man pulling back with his left shoulder and hand, causing an awkward angle of motion.
11. Woman leaning heavily on partner's arm.

Trends in Vocabulary and Leading

The closed dance position is presently being referred to as the *frame.* The term conjures a body position of substance, firmness, or presence as opposed to "limp" or "just there!" In addition, the terms "man and lady" or "man and woman" are being replaced by "leader" and "follower." Further, the traditional "women follow–men lead" notion is being reversed but not because of gender imbalance! The reversal is used to stimulate sensitivity to a partner's responsibilities. Switching roles, albeit temporary, should improve a dancer's ability to lead or to follow.

Techniques of Leading and Following

Leading is done primarily by the use of the body, arms, and hands. The man sets the rhythm, decides what steps are to be used, and controls the direction and progression around the floor. The woman is completely dependent upon her partner. Therefore, an alert yet easy posture should be assumed to allow dancers to move as a unit. The firmness of the man's hand on the woman's back is an important pressure lead for changes in dance position and direction. Through the use of gently yet firm leads, the man can make dancing a mutually pleasant experience.

The woman's responsibility is to follow her partner and adapt to any rhythm or style. She should maintain an easy resistance to give the man an alert, movable partner to lead. The woman should always maintain contact with her partner's upper right arm and shoulder and give firm resistance to his hand on her back. Should the man be a poor leader, the woman must then pay close attention to his body movement, particularly the shoulders and chest, in order to follow. When in a position apart from a partner, following requires a firm controlled arm that responds to a lead by simultaneous action of the body. In the challenge position, the woman's only lead is visual. She must be alert and follow her partner's action by watching him. Some general rules for following are: (a) keep the man's rhythm and be alert to his leads; (b) support one's own weight; (c) step straight back with a reaching motion to give partner room to step straight ahead; (d) feet should pass close together; (e) know the basic steps and leads; (f) try not to anticipate

DANCE POSITIONS

1. Back Cross

2. Butterfly

3. Challenge or Shine

4. Closed

5. Conversation

6. Escort

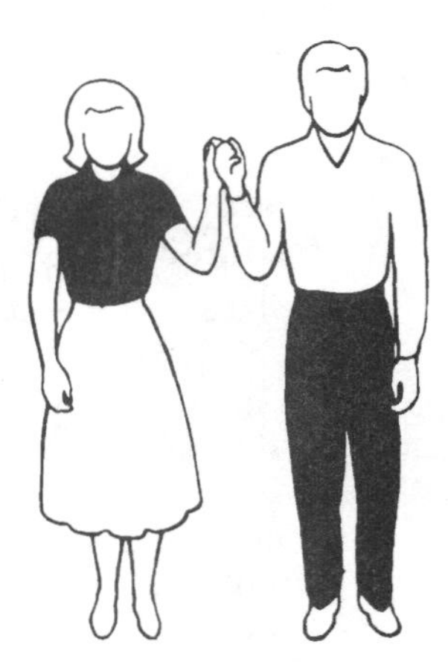

7. Inside Hands Joined. Side by Side. Couple

8. Left Parallel. Side Car

9. Open

10. Pigeon Wing

Detailed description for each position is given in the Glossary.

DANCE POSITIONS (con't)

11. Promenade, Skaters

12. Reverse Open

13. Reverse Varsouvienne

14. Right Parallel. Swing, Banjo

15. Semiopen

16. Shoulder-Waist

17. Swing Out. Flirtation

18. Two Hands Joined. Facing

19. Varsouvienne Jody

20. Wrap

partner's action; (g) work on maintaining proper body alignment and good easy posture.

SPECIFIC DIRECTIONS FOR LEADING

1. **To lead the first step,** the man should precede the step off with the left foot by an upbeat, forward motion of the body.
2. **To lead a forward moving pattern,** the man should give a forward motion in the body, including the right arm, which will direct the woman firmly in the desired direction.
3. **To lead a backward moving pattern,** the man should use pressure of the right hand. This will draw the woman forward in the desired direction.
4. **To lead a sideward moving pattern in closed position,** the man should use pressure of the right hand to the left or right to indicate the desired direction.
5. **To lead a box step,** the man should use a forward body action followed by right-hand pressure and right-elbow pull to the right to take the woman into the forward sequence of the box. Forward pressure of the right hand followed by pressure to the left side takes her into the back sequence of the box.
6. **To lead a box turn,** with slight pressure of the right hand, the man should use the right arm and shoulder to guide or bank her into the turn. The shoulders press forward during the forward step and draw backward during the backward step.
7. **To lead into an open position,** or conversation position, the man should use pressure with the heel of the hand to turn the woman into open position. The right elbow lowers to the side. The man must simultaneously turn his own body, not just the woman, so that they end facing the same direction. The left arm relaxes slightly and the left hand sometimes gives the lead for steps in open position.
8. **To lead from open to closed position,** the man should use pressure of the right hand and raise the right arm up to standard position to move the woman into closed position. She should not have to be pushed, but should swing easily into closed position as she feels the arm lifting. She should come clear around to face the man squarely.
9. **To lead into right parallel position** (left reverse open position), the man should not use pressure of his right hand, but rather should raise his right arm, rotating her counterclockwise one-eighth of a turn while he rotates counterclockwise one-eighth of a turn. This places the man and the woman off to the side of each other, facing opposite directions. The woman is to the right of him but slightly in front of him. The man should avoid turning too far so as to be side by side as this results in poor style and awkward and uncomfortable motion. The man's left hand may assist the lead by pulling toward his left shoulder.
10. **To lead from right parallel position to left parallel position,** the man should pull with his right hand, lowering the right arm, and push slightly with his left hand causing a rotation clockwise about a quarter turn until the woman is to the left of him but slightly in front of him. They are not side by side.
11. **To lead a hesitation step,** the man should use pressure of the right hand on the first step and sudden body tension to control a hold of position as long as desired.
12. **To lead all turns,** the man dips his shoulder in the direction of the turn, and his upper torso turns before his leg and foot turn.
13. **To lead into a pivot turn,** clockwise, the man should hold the woman slightly closer, but with sudden body tension. Resistance is exerted outward by both the man and woman leaning away from each other in order to take advantage of the centrifugal force of the circular motion. The right foot steps between partner's feet, forward on the line of direction, while the left foot reaches across the line of direction and turns on the ball of the foot about three-quarters of the way around.
14. **To lead into a corté** (dip) the man should use firm pressure of the right hand with sudden increased body tension going into the preparation step. Then the man should draw his partner forward toward him as he steps back into the dip. The left foot taking the dip backward should carry the weight, and careful balance of the weight should remain over that foot. Pressure is released as they recover to the other foot.
15. **Finger pressure leads and arm control** are important. Many times the man's only contact with his partner is with one hand or changing from hand to hand. A soft, gentle hand hold

and a limp arm make it impossible to lead the variations of Swing, Cha Cha Cha, or Rumba. It is necessary that the woman exert slight resistance to the man's grasp so that pressure in any direction is reacted to instantly. Both man and woman should maintain elbow control by holding the arm firmly in front of the body with elbows down and always slightly bent. The arm is seldom allowed to extend in the elbow as this destroys the spring action needed to move out and in and under without jerking. The fingers often need to slip around the partner's without actually losing contact, in order to maintain comfortable action of the wrist and arm.

16. **To change the rhythm pattern,** the man exerts extra pressure with the right hand and pushes a little harder from the chest.
17. **Visual lead.** When partners are apart, as in the shine position of Cha Cha Cha, the woman watches her partner closely.

Following

The woman's responsibility in dancing is to follow her partner and adapt to any rhythm or style he dances. She should maintain an easy resistance (not rigidity or tension) throughout the body that gives the man an alert, movable partner whom he can lead. If the woman is too relaxed or too light, leading becomes very difficult, for there is no resistance. In other words, it takes cooperation for two people to dance well, the same way it takes two people for a satisfactory handshake. The woman should always maintain contact with her partner's upper right arm and shoulder and give resistance against his hand at her back, moving with it as it guides her. If the man is a poor leader, then the woman must pay close attention to his body movement, particularly his chest and shoulder movement, in order to follow. Following, when in an apart position, requires a firm, controlled arm that responds to a lead by simultaneous action of the body. A limp arm with no resultant body response makes leading difficult in Swing, Rumba, and Cha Cha Cha. In the challenge position, the woman's only lead is visual. She must be alert and follow her partner's action by watching him. The good dancer will aim to dance with beauty of form. The woman can make a poor dancer look good or a good dancer look excellent. She can also cramp his style if she takes too small a step, has poor control of balance, dances with her feet apart, dances at an awkward angle, or leans forward.

GENERAL RULES FOR FOLLOWING

1. Keep the man's rhythm.
2. Be alert to partner's lead
3. Support one's own weight. Arch the back and move with the partner's hand.
4. Step straight backward with reaching motion so as to give the partner room to step straight ahead.
5. Pass the feet close together.
6. Know the basic steps and basic leads.
7. Try not to anticipate partner's action, just move with it.
8. Give careful thought to proper body alignment and good posture.

RHYTHM AND METER

Rhythm

Rhythm is the regular pattern of movement and/or sound. It is a relationship between time and force factors. It is felt, seen, or heard.

Beat

Beat is the basic unit that measures time. The duration of time becomes established by the beat, or the pulse, as it is repeated. It is referred to as the **underlying beat.**

Accent

Accent is the stress placed on a beat to make it stronger or louder than the others. The primary accent is on the first beat of the music. There may be a secondary accent.

When the accent is placed on the unnatural beat (the off beat), the rhythm is syncopated.

Measure

A *measure* is one group of beats made by the regular occurrence of the heavy accent. It represents the underlying beat enclosed between two adjacent bars on a musical staff.

Meter

Meter is the metric division of a measure into parts of equal time value and regular accents. Meter can be recognized by listening for the accent on the first beat.

Time Signature

Time signature is a symbol (e.g., 2/4) that establishes the duration of time. The upper number indicates the number of beats per measure, and the lower number indicates the note value that receives one beat.

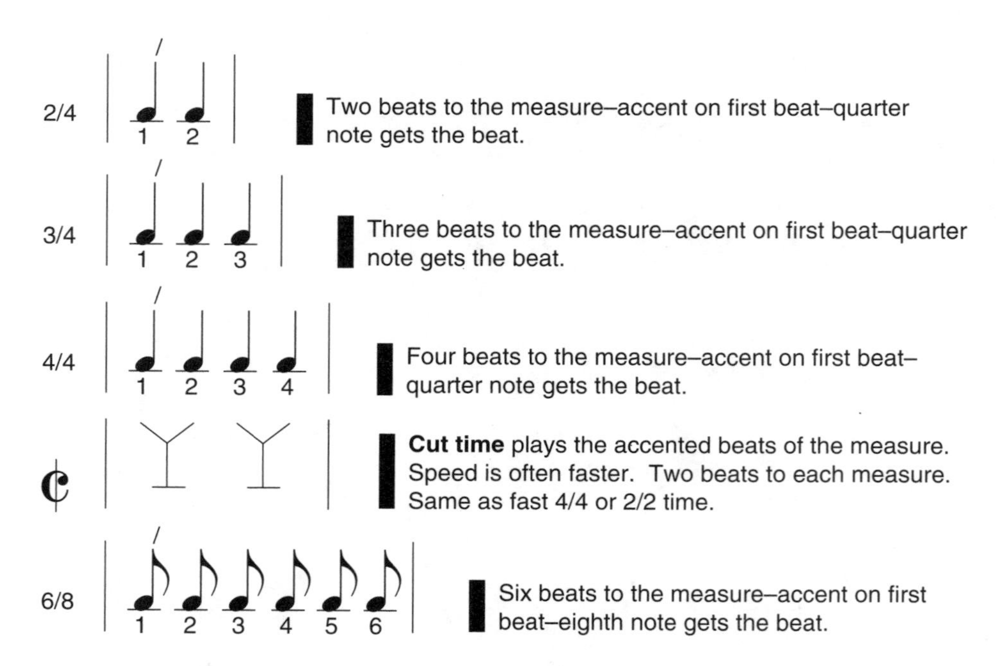

Note Values

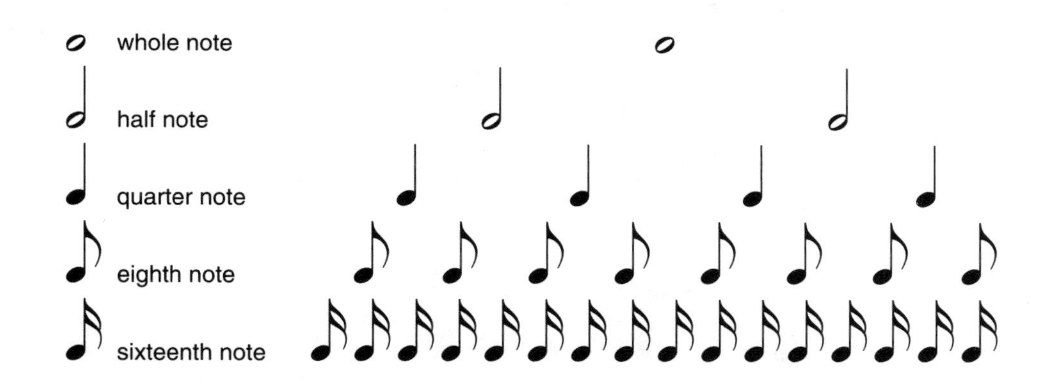

or

dotted quarter or dotted eighth notes
A *dotted note* increases the value by one-half. Therefore the dotted note equals one and a half value of the original symbol. A dotted quarter note, then, is equal to a quarter plus an eighth; a dotted eighth is equal to an eighth plus sixteenth.

triplet
A group of three notes played in the usual time of two similar notes. It would be counted *one-and-a* for one quarter note.

Line Values

Whereas the musical notation establishes the *relative value of beats,* these same relative values can be represented by lines:

one whole note ________________________________

two half notes _______________ _______________

four quarter notes _______ _______ _______ _______

eight eighth notes ___ ___ ___ ___ ___ ___ ___ ___

sixteen sixteenth notes _ _ _ _ _ _ _ _ _ _ _ _ _ _ _ _

Phrase

A musical sentence, or *phrase,* can be felt by listening for a complete thought. This can be a group of measures, generally four or eight measures. A group of phrases can express a group of complete thoughts that are related just as a group of sentences expresses a group of complete thoughts in a paragraph. Groups of phrases are generally 16 to 32 measures long.

Tempo

Tempo is the rate of speed at which music is played. Tempo influences the mood or the quality of music and movement. Sometimes at the beginning of the music or the dance, the tempo is established by a metronome reading. For example, metronome 128 means the equal recurrence of beats at the rate of 128 per minute.

Rhythm Pattern

The *rhythm pattern* is the grouping of beats that repeat for the pattern of a dance step, just as for the melody of a song. The rhythm pattern must correspond to the underlying beat. Example: meter or underlying beat 4/4.

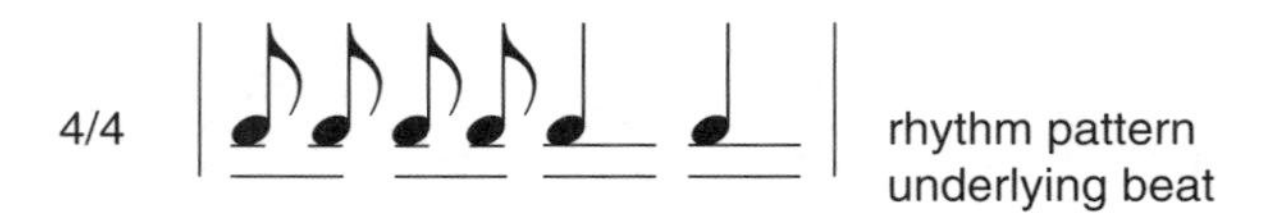

Even Rhythm

When the beats in the rhythm pattern are all the same value (note or line value)–all long (slow) or all short (quick)–the rhythm is **even.** Examples: walk, run, hop, jump, leap, Waltz, Schottische.

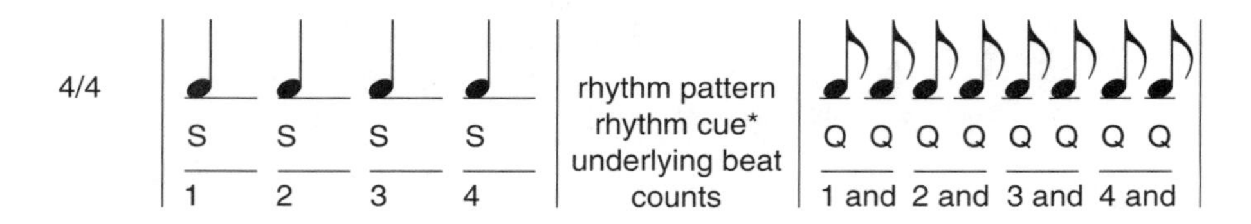

Uneven Rhythm

When the beats in the rhythm pattern are not all the same value, but are any combination of slow and quick beats, the rhythm is **uneven.** Examples: Two-Step, Foxtrot.

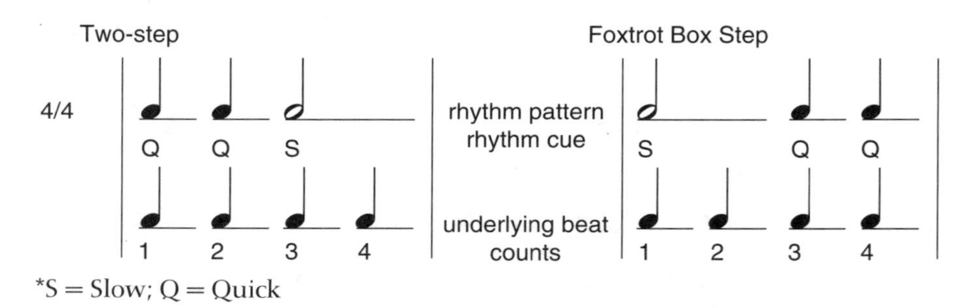

*S = Slow; Q = Quick

A *dotted beat* borrows half the value of itself again. Examples: skip, slide, gallop.

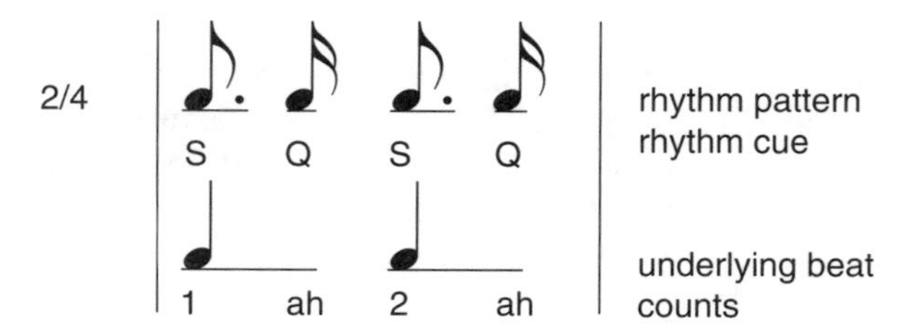

When the note comes before the bar, it is called a *pick-up beat.*

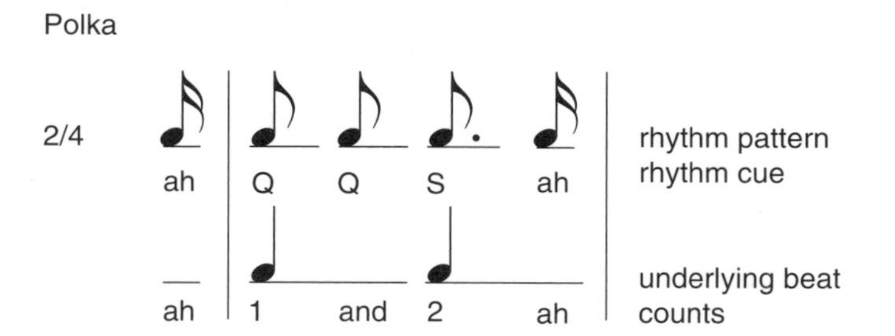

Broken Rhythm

Broken rhythm is a combination of slow and quick beats when the rhythm pattern takes more than one measure. A repetition begins in the middle of the measure. Example: Magic Step in the Foxtrot.

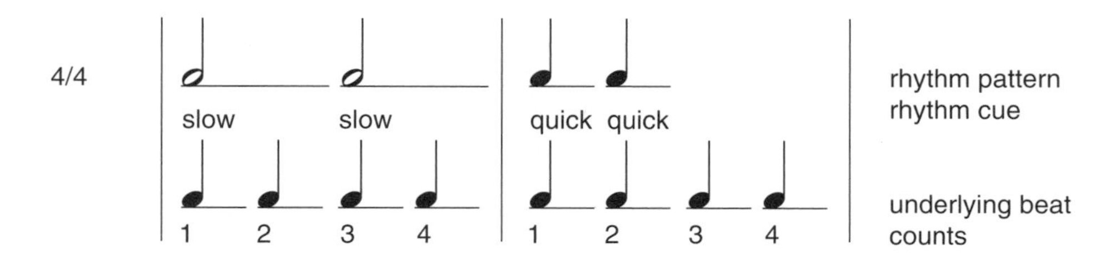

ANALYSIS OF A BASIC RHYTHM

A teacher should thoroughly understand the complete analysis of each basic dance step to be taught. The following example shows the eight related parts of an analysis. Each basic dance step has been analyzed in this manner (including the basic steps of Social Dance).

Two-Step

				same
				meter 2/4
	/			accent
2/4	step	close	step	step pattern
				rhythm pattern
	quick	quick	slow	rhythm cue
				underlying beat
	1	and	2	counts
		uneven rhythm		type of rhythm

BASIC DANCE STEPS

Shuffle, Dance Walk, or Glide

1. An easy, light step, from one foot to the other, in even rhythm.
2. Different from a walk in that the weight is over the ball of the foot.
3. The feet remain lightly in contact with the floor.

■ *Two-Step*

1. 2/4 or 4/4 meter.
2. Uneven rhythm.
3. Step forward on left foot, close right to left, take weight on right, step left again. Repeat, beginning with right.
4. The rhythm is quick, quick, slow.

2/4	/ step	close	step
	L	R	L
	Q	Q	S
	1	and	2

uneven rhythm

■ *Waltz*

1. 3/4 meter–accent first beat.
2. A smooth, graceful dance step in even rhythm.
3. Consists of three steps; step forward on the left, step to the side with the right, close left to right, take weight on left.

3/4	/ fwd	side	close	fwd	side	close
	L	R	L	R	L	R
	S	S	S	S	S	S
	1	2	3	1	2	3

even rhythm

4. The **Box Waltz** is the basic pattern for the Box Waltz turn. Step left forward, step right sideward, passing close to the left foot, close left to right, taking weight left; step right backward, step left sideward, passing close to the right foot, close right to left, take weight right. *Cue:* Forward side close, back side close.

3/4	/ fwd	side	close	back	side	close
	L	R	L	R	L	R
	S	S	S	S	S	S
	1	2	3	1	2	3

even rhythm

5. The **Running Waltz** used so often in European Folk Dances is a tiny three-beat running step with an accent on the first beat, three beats to each measure.

6. **Canter Waltz** rhythm is an uneven rhythm in Waltz time with the action taking place on beats one and three. The rhythm is slow, quick; slow, quick or long, short. (Refer to Canter rhythm, p. 69.)

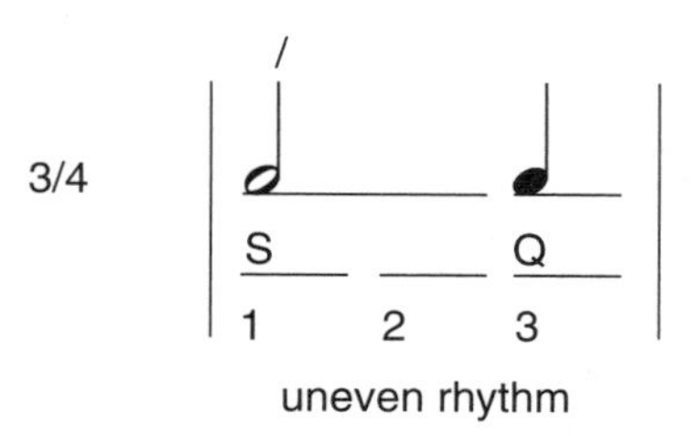

BASIC DANCE TURNS

Using the fundamental dance steps, partners may turn clockwise or counterclockwise. Basically, if the man is leading with the left, the turn is counterclockwise; if he is leading with the right, the turn is clockwise. But in Folk Dance, the majority of the partner turns are clockwise. A successful turn actually starts with the preceding step, the man's back to center and his body moving into the turn. The man steps left backward in the line of direction, which allows his right foot to lead on the second step.

■ *Two-Step Turn Clockwise*

The Two-Step rhythm is uneven 2/4 or 4/4 meter with a quick-quick-slow pattern. There is a half-turn on each measure (2/4 meter). The starting position is closed, with the man's back to center of the circle. *The turn is on the second count.*

Left-Foot Sequence (Man)

Count 1 — Step left sideward.
Count and — Close right to left, taking weight on right.
Count 2 — Step left around partner, toeing in and pivoting clockwise on the ball of the foot a half-turn around.

Right-Foot Sequence (Woman)

Count 1 — Step right sideward.
Count and — Close left to right, taking weight on left.
Count 2 — Step right forward between partner's feet and pivoting clockwise on the ball of the foot a half-turn around.

■ NOTE

The man starts with the left sequence, the woman starts with the right sequence. After a half-turn, the woman then starts with the left sequence and the man with the right sequence. They continue to alternate. By this process of *dovetailing with the feet,* man and woman can turn easily without stepping on each other's feet. Couple progresses in the line of direction as they turn.

■ STYLE

The steps should be small and close to partner. The body leans back and aids in the turn. The turn is on the ball of the foot. Each partner must give the impetus for the turn by pivoting on his or her own foot.

▪ LEAD

Closed position, the man should have a firm right hand on the small of the woman's back so that she can lean back against it. His right arm guides her as he turns.

▪ CUES

1. Left-Foot sequence: side close around.
   Right-Foot sequence: side close between.
2. Practicing together in closed position.
   Side close turn, side close turn.

Waltz Turn

The Waltz rhythm is even 3/4 meter. Three patterns are presented: the Box Waltz, traditional step-side-close, and Running Waltz pattern.

▪ BOX WALTZ TURN—CLOCKWISE, COUNTERCLOCKWISE

The Box Waltz turn is used in social dancing and in some American Folk Dances and can go either to the left in a counterclockwise turn or to the right in a clockwise turn, depending on which foot leads the turn. (These turns are described under the Waltz box turn, pp. 70–71.)

▪ CLOCKWISE TURN

The clockwise turn is the turn most often used for Folk Dances. Two patterns are presented, the first based on the traditional step-side-close pattern and the second on the running Waltz pattern. It is in 3/4 meter.

▪ STEP-SIDE-CLOSE PATTERN (TRADITIONAL)

Left-Foot Sequence (Man). Step left around partner, pivoting on the ball of the foot a half-turn clockwise (count 1). Step right sideward in line of direction (count 2). Close left to right, take weight left (count 3).

Right-Foot Sequence (Woman). Step right forward between partner's feet, pivoting on the ball of the foot a half-turn clockwise (count 1). Step left sideward in the line of direction (count 2). Close right to left, take weight right (count 3).

▪ NOTE

The man starts with the left sequence, the woman with the right sequence. After a half-turn the woman starts with the left sequence and the man with the right sequence. They continue to alternate. By this process of dovetailing the feet, dancers can turn easily without stepping on each other's feet.

▪ STYLE

The steps are small and close to partner. The pivot halfway around is on the ball of the foot on the first count. Each partner is responsible for supplying the impetus for the ball of the foot turn.

▪ LEAD

The man has a firm right hand at the woman's back. She leans back and is guided into the turn by his firm right hand and arm.

▪ CUES

1. Left-foot sequence: around side close.
   Right-foot sequence: between side close.
2. Practice together in closed position.
   Turn side close, turn side close.

▪ STEP-STEP-CLOSE PATTERN

Left-Foot Sequence (Man). Step left in the line of direction (toeing in, heel leads), pivoting on the ball of the foot and starting a half-turn clockwise (count 1). Take two small steps, right, left, close to first step, completing half-turn (counts 2 and 3).

Right-Foot Sequence (Woman). Step right in line of direction (toeing out) *between partner's feet,* pivoting on the ball of the foot, starting a half-turn clockwise (count 1). Take two small steps, left, right, close to first step, completing half-turn (counts 2 and 3).

▪ NOTE

1. When the man steps backward left, the right foot leads the clockwise turn.
2. The man starts with the left sequence, the woman with the right sequence. After a half-turn, the woman starts with the left sequence and the man with the right sequence. They continue to alternate. When doing left-foot sequence, step backward in line of direction; when doing the right-foot sequence, step forward (but not as long a step as the first step in the other sequence). The dancers are turning on each count, but steps on counts 2 and 3 are almost in place. *Both feet are together on count 3.*

▪ LEAD

The man has a firm right hand at the woman's back. She leans back and is guided into the turn by his firm right hand and arm.

▪ CUES

Left-Foot sequence: Back turn turn.
Right-Foot sequence: Forward turn turn.

▪ REVERSE DIRECTION OF TURN

If turning counterclockwise, the left foot leads. If turning clockwise, the right foot leads. To change leads from left to right or right to left, one measure (3 beats) is needed for transition. A balance step backward or one Waltz step forward facilitates the transition. Or turning counterclockwise, after a left Waltz step, immediately reverse direction with a right Waltz step, turning clockwise (a more difficult maneuver). Eventually the lead comes back to a left one, and another transition occurs.

2 Ballroom Favorites

Foxtrot

The Foxtrot, as a present-day form, is of relatively recent origin. The only truly American form of Ballroom Dance, it has had many steps and variations through the years. The Foxtrot gets its name from a musical comedy star, Henry Fox, of the years 1913–1914 (Hostetler 1952), who danced a fast but simple trotting step to ragtime music in one of the Ziegfeld shows of that time. As an additional publicity stunt, the theater management requested that a star nightclub performer, Oscar Duryea, introduce the step to the public but found that it had to be modified somewhat, because a continuous trotting step could not be maintained for long periods without exhausting effort. Duryea simplified the step so that it became four walking steps alternating with eight quick running steps. This was the first Foxtrot.

Since that time, under the influence of Vernon and Irene Castle and a series of professional dancers, the Foxtrot has been through a gradual refining process and has developed into a beautifully smooth dance. It claims considerable popularity today.

Music from ragtime through the blues on down to modern jazz and swing has had its effect on the Foxtrot. The original Foxtrot was danced to a lively 2/4 rhythm. Its two parent forms were the One-Step, 2/4 – – – – quick quick quick quick rhythm; the other was the Two-Step, 2/4 | – – – | – – – | quick quick slow or step-close-step. Both of these forms are danced today but have given way to a slower, smoother 4/4 time and a more streamlined style. The Foxtrot is danced in three tempos (slow, medium, and fast) and can be adapted to almost any tempo played in the music.

The basic Foxtrot steps can be used together in any combination or sequence. A dancer who knows the basic steps and understands the fundamentals of rhythm can make up his or her own combinations easily and gradually develop the possibilities for variation in position, direction, and tempo.

FOXTROT RHYTHM

The modern Foxtrot in 4/4 time, or cut time, has four quarter beats or their equivalent to each measure. Each beat is given the same amount of time, but there is an accent on the first and third beats of the measure. When a step is taken on each beat (1–2–3–4), these are called *quick beats.* When steps are taken only on the two accented bets (1 and 3), they are twice as long and are called *slow beats.*

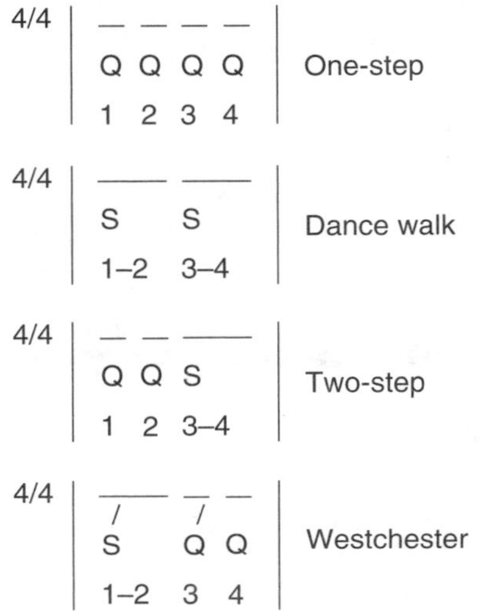

```
4/4 | — — — —   |
    | Q Q Q Q   |  One-step
    | 1 2 3 4   |

4/4 | ——— ———   |
    | S   S     |  Dance walk
    | 1–2 3–4   |

4/4 | — — ———   |
    | Q Q S     |  Two-step
    | 1 2 3–4   |

4/4 | ——— — —   |
    |  /  /     |
    | S   Q Q   |  Westchester
    | 1–2 3 4   |
```

A use of these quick and slow beats and a combination of them into rhythm patterns form the basis for all of the modern Foxtrot steps. There are two patterns used predominantly: the magic step and the Westchester box step.

Magic Step

The magic step pattern represents broken rhythm as it takes a measure and half of music and may be repeated from the middle of the measure. It is an uneven rhythm pattern, slow slow quick quick.

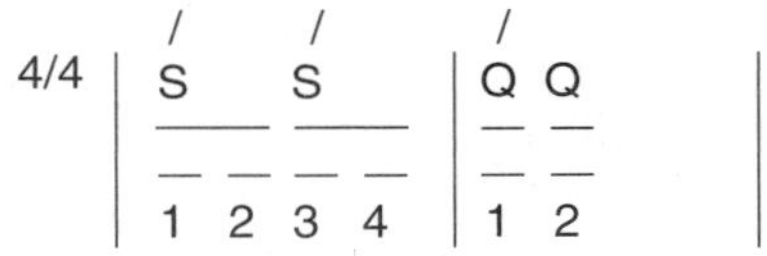

```
     /   /      /
4/4 | S   S    | Q Q  |
    | ——— ———  | — —  |
    | — — — —  | — —  |
    | 1 2 3 4  | 1 2  |
```

uneven rhythm
Magic step

■ *Westchester Box Step*

The Westchester box step is a one-measure pattern, but it takes two measures to complete the box. The rhythm is uneven, slow quick quick. The rhythm may also be played in cut time, but it is still slow quick quick. Beats 1 and 2 are put together to make 1 beat. Beats 3 and 4 are put together to make 1 beat. The time signature for cut time is ¢. It is played faster and feels very much like 2/4 time.

Cut-time is based on 4/4 time

4/4 | 1 2 3 4 |

¢ | Y Y |

Westchester box step ¢ time

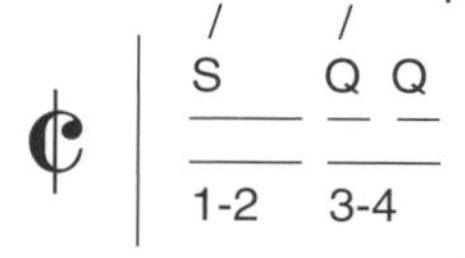

uneven rhythm

FOXTROT STYLE

Foxtrot style truly reflects its American origin. It is the least affected of any of the Ballroom Dances. Completely without stylized or eccentric arm, foot, head, or torso movement, the Foxtrot is a beautifully smooth dance. The body is held easily erect and follows the foot pattern in a relaxed way with little up and down or sideward movement. The good dancer glides normally along the floor and blends the various steps together without bobbing or jerking. This effect is accomplished by long, reaching steps with only as much knee bend as is needed to transfer the weight smoothly from step to step. It gives the Foxtrot a streamlined motion and a simple beauty of form that can be enjoyed without strain or fatigue, dance after dance. As one becomes more and more skillful at putting together steps for the Foxtrot, there will be increasing joy derived from the tremendous variety of quick and slow combinations.

FUNDAMENTAL FOXTROT STEPS

Directions are for man, facing line of direction; woman's part is reversed, except when noted.

■ *Introductory Steps*

■ ONE-STEP

(Closed position)

STEPS	4/4 COUNTS	RHYTHM CUE
Step L forward	1	quick
Step R forward	2	quick
Step L forward	3	quick
Step R forward	4	quick

STYLE: It is like a regular walk, heel first.

Step L backward	1	quick
Step R backward	2	quick
Step L backward	3	quick
Step R backward	4	quick

STYLE: Reach straight back with toe of foot.

NOTE: Refer to detailed analysis of One-Step, p. 5.

Fundamental Foxtrot Steps (continued)

■ **TURN**

Counterclockwise (L) step on each beat (L, R, L, R) in place.

VARIATION: Alternate 4 quick and 4 slow. Try different combination of rhythms, moving forward, backward, turning, and sideward.

■ **DANCE WALK**

(Forward or backward*) (Closed position)

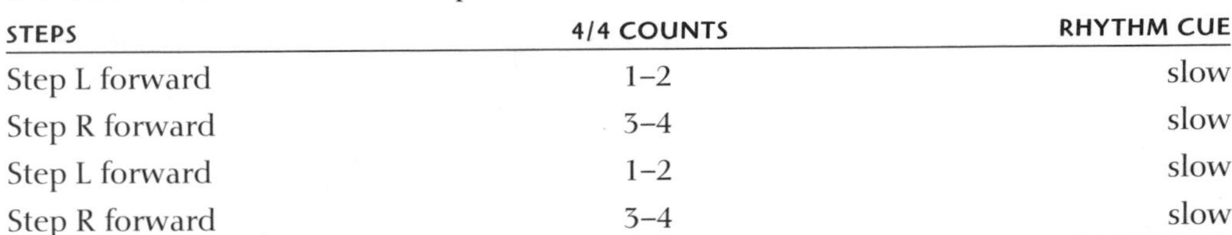

STEPS	4/4 COUNTS	RHYTHM CUE
Step L forward	1–2	slow
Step R forward	3–4	slow
Step L forward	1–2	slow
Step R forward	3–4	slow

STYLE: It is like a regular walk, heel first, but should be a long, smooth, reaching motion.

Step L backward	1–2	slow
Step R backward	3–4	slow
Step L backward	1–2	slow
Step R backward	3–4	slow

STYLE: It is a long, smooth, reaching motion to the toe of the foot, straight back.

LEAD: A basic position that gives security and support.

NOTE: Refer to detailed analysis of Dance Walk, p. 5.

■ **SIDE CLOSE**

(Chasse; a sideward-moving step) (Closed position)

STEPS	4/4 COUNTS	RHYTHM CUE
Step L sideward	1	quick
Step R to L, take weight on R	2	quick

STYLE: Steps should be short, smooth, sideward motion, on the ball of the foot.

LEAD: Knowledge of cues used to lead specific positions or directions.

NOTE: Repetition of this step will continue action to man's left.

■ *Magic Step Series*

Magic Step (Basic step)	Right and Left Parallel	Pivot Turn
Open Magic Step	The Conversation Pivot	
Magic Left Turn	The Corté	

The magic step series was created by Arthur Murray (1954). It is called by this name because it can be varied in a surprising number of ways. The pattern is uneven rhythm and requires a measure and a half for one basic step. This is called broken rhythm.

■ **MAGIC STEP**

(Basic Step) (Closed position)

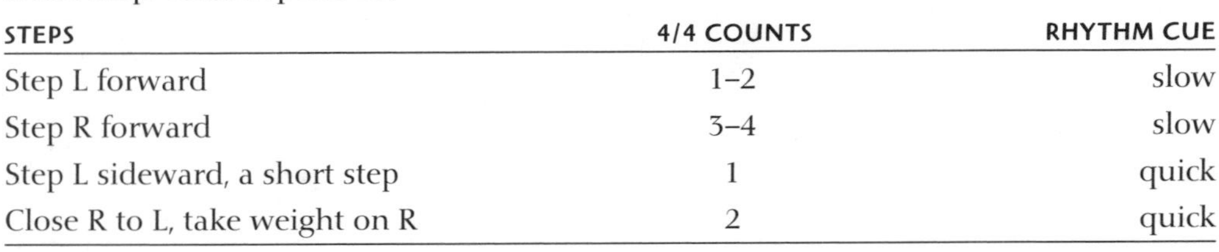

STEPS	4/4 COUNTS	RHYTHM CUE
Step L forward	1–2	slow
Step R forward	3–4	slow
Step L sideward, a short step	1	quick
Close R to L, take weight on R	2	quick

STEP CUE:	forward forward	side close	Floor pattern
	long steps	short steps	start

STYLE: The forward steps should be long, smooth, walking steps, straight ahead. The woman, moving backward, takes a long step reaching from hip to toe.

LEAD: A body and right arm lead forward.

VARIATIONS ON THE MAGIC STEP PATTERN: The following three techniques are used for maneuvering in a closed dance position.

1. Forward or backward–the man may maneuver forward or backward if he is aware of the traffic around him. The lead to move backward is a pressure lead at the woman's back during the quick quick beats and then a step into the backward direction on the next slow beat. Generally the man will not have room to move backward more than one or two consecutive patterns.
2. Right or left–the man may maneuver to the right or to the left to go around another couple. He will change direction on the quick quick beats by use of a pressure lead with his right hand and turn his body at the same time one-eighth of a turn to the right so as to travel diagonally outward or one-eighth turn to the left so as to travel diagonally inward beginning with the next slow beat. The right turn is particularly handy in leading a partner out of a crowded situation away from the center of the floor. Closed position is retained throughout.
3. Dance in place–used on a crowded dance floor. Closed dance position:

STEPS	4/4 COUNTS	RHYTHM CUE
Step sideward L, slide R to L, no weight change	1–2	slow
Step sideward R, slide L to R, no weight change	3–4	slow
Step sideward L	1	quick
Close R to L, take weight R	2	quick

STEP CUE: Step slide, step slide, quick quick.

STYLE: The steps are very small.

LEAD: Increase pressure with the right hand to keep the woman from stepping back. Indicate sideward action.

NOTE: The man may maneuver this in-place pattern into a turn counterclockwise by the use of the right hand and elbow.

■ OPEN MAGIC STEP

(Closed position)

STEPS	4/4 COUNTS	RHYTHM CUE
Step L forward	1–2	slow
Step R forward	3–4	slow
Step L forward a short step, turning to open dance position	1	quick
Close R to L, take weight R	2	quick
Step L forward in open position	3–4	slow
Step R forward	1–2	slow
Step L forward a short step	3	quick
Close R to L, take weight R	4	quick

Fundamental Foxtrot Steps (continued)

Step L forward	1–2	slow
Step R forward	3–4	slow
Step L forward a short step, turning to closed position	1	quick
Close R to L, take weight R	2	quick

STEP CUE: Slow slow quick quick.

STYLE: It is a heel lead on the slow beats in open position for both the man and woman.

LEAD: To lead into an open position or conversation position, the man should use pressure with the heel of the right hand to turn the woman into open position. The right elbow lowers to the side. The man must simultaneously turn his own body, not just the woman so that they end facing the same direction. The left arm relaxes slightly and the left hand sometimes gives the lead for steps in the open position.

LEAD: To lead from open to closed position the man should use pressure of the right hand and raise the right arm up to standard position to move the woman into closed position. The woman should not have to be pushed but should swing easily into closed position as she feels the arm lifting. She should move completely around to face the man squarely.

LEAD: The man may wish to return to closed position on the quick beats following the first two slows in open position.

NOTE: It is possible to maneuver when going into open position so that the couple opens facing the line of direction and afterward closes with the man still facing the line of direction, starting from closed position as follows:

STEPS	4/4 COUNTS	RHYTHM CUE
Step L forward	1–2	slow
Step R forward	3–4	slow
Step L, R moving around the woman on the L side while turning her halfway around to open position	1–2	quick, quick
Step L forward in open position moving in line of direction	3–4	slow
Step R forward	1–2	slow
Step L, R in place, bringing the woman around to face the closed dance position	3–4	quick quick

STEP CUE: Slow slow come around/slow slow in place.

STYLE: The woman must be sure to swing around, facing the man, into a correct closed dance position while taking two quick beats.

LEAD: The man must start bringing his right elbow up to indicate to the woman that he is going into closed position on the first quick beat.

NOTE: Any number of open magic steps may be done consecutively when traveling in the line of direction without fear of interfering with the dancing of other couples.

■ MAGIC LEFT TURN

(Closed position)

STEPS	4/4 COUNTS	RHYTHM CUE
Step L forward a short step	1–2	slow
Step R backward, toe in and turn counterclockwise one-quarter	3–4	slow
Step in place L, toeing out L, and turning one-quarter counterclockwise	1	quick
Step R to L, take weight R, and finish the one-half turn	2	quick
Repeat to make a full turn.		

STEP CUE: Rock rock step close.
S S Q Q

STYLE: The slow steps forward and backward are like short rocking steps, but the body is straight, not leaning.

LEAD: The man must strongly increase pressure at the woman's back on the first step so that she will not swing her left foot backward. Then he uses his firm right arm to turn her with him counterclockwise. As the woman reacts to these two leads, she will step in between the man's feet and pivot on her left foot as he guides her around.

NOTE: The pattern may be reduced to a quarter-turn at a time, or it may be increased to make a full turn at a time. This variation provides a means of turning in place or of turning to maneuver into position for another variation or for recovering the original line of direction. Because of this, it is often used to tie together all types of Foxtrot variations.

▪ RIGHT AND LEFT PARALLEL MAGIC STEP

(Closed position)

This is a delightful variation involving right and left parallel position.

STEPS	4/4 COUNTS	RHYTHM CUE
Step forward	1–2	slow
Step R forward	3–4	slow
Step L sideward a short step, turning to R parallel position	1	quick
Close R to L, take weight on R	2	quick
Step forward L, diagonally in R parallel position	3–4	slow
Step forward R	1–2	slow
Step in place L, turning in place one-quarter clockwise into L parallel position	3	quick
Close R to L, take weight on R	4	quick
Step forward L in L parallel position	1–2	slow
Step forward R	3–4	slow
Step in place L, turning to R parallel	1	quick
Close R to L, take weight on R	2	quick
Step L forward in R parallel position	3–4	slow
Step R forward	1–2	slow
Step L in place, turning to closed position	3	quick
Close R to L, take weight on R	4	quick

STEP CUE: Slow slow quick quick.

STYLE: The woman in parallel position must reach back parallel to the man's forward reach.

LEAD: To lead into right parallel position the man should not use pressure of his right hand but rather should raise his right arm rotating the woman counterclockwise one-eighth of a turn while he rotates counterclockwise one-eighth of a turn. This places the man and woman off to the side of each other facing opposite directions. The woman is to the right of the man but slightly in front of him. The man should avoid turning too far so as to be side by side as this results in poor style and awkward and uncomfortable motion. The man's left hand may assist the lead by pulling toward his left shoulder.

Fundamental Foxtrot Steps (continued)

LEAD: To lead from right parallel position to left parallel position, the man should pull with his right hand lowering the right arm and push slightly with his left hand causing a rotation clockwise about a quarter of a turn until the woman is to the left of him but slightly in front of him. They are not side by side.

NOTE: The couple should move forward in a zigzag pattern, down the floor, changing from one parallel position to the other. The man must be careful to take the quick beats in place as he is changing position in order to make a smooth transition. A more advanced use of this variation is to make a half-turn clockwise in place on the quick beats as the man changes from right parallel position to left parallel position so that the man would then travel backward in the line of direction and the woman forward. A half-turn counterclockwise in place would then turn the couple back to right parallel position. Innumerable combinations of this variation will develop as dancers experiment with changes of direction.

▪ THE CONVERSATION PIVOT

(Open position)

STEPS	4/4 COUNTS	RHYTHM CUE
Step L forward	1–2	slow
Step R forward	3–4	slow
Step L around the woman clockwise going into closed position	1–2	slow
Step R between woman's feet and pivot on the R foot, turning clockwise	3–4	slow
Step L forward a short step, taking open position again	1	quick
Close R to L, taking weight R	2	quick

NOTE: Two extra slow beats have been added for this variation, S S S S Q Q.

STEP CUE: Step step pivot pivot quick quick.

STYLE: Couples must hold the body firmly and press outward to move with the centrifugal force of the motion on the pivot turn. The woman will step forward in between the man's feet on the third slow beat and then around him with her left foot on the fourth slow beat, followed by a quick quick to balance oneself in place.

LEAD: See lead indication above. The pivot turn is only the third and fourth slow beats. Then the man will lead into open position and take the quick beats.

NOTE: Following this variation it is usually wise to dance one more magic step in open position before leading into the basic closed position. Note details on pivot turn, pp. 32–34.

▪ THE CORTÉ

(A fascinating dip step in magic step rhythm) (Closed position)

STEPS	4/4 COUNTS	RHYTHM CUE
Step L forward	1–2	slow
Step R forward	3–4	slow
Step L sideward a short step	1	quick
Close R to L, take weight on R	2	quick
Dip L backward	3–4	slow
Transfer weight forward onto R foot	1–2	slow
Step L sideward, a short step	3	quick
Close R to L, take weight R	4	quick

STEP CUE: Slow slow	quick quick (preparation beats)	dip (corté)	recover quick quick. (weight forward)

STYLE: *Man*–The weight is transferred onto the left foot as the man steps backward into the dip. The left knee is bent, the back is straight, the right toe extends forward. *Woman*–Her weight is transferred onto the right foot as she steps forward into the dip.The right knee is bent and directly over her foot. The back is arched, keeping her straight up and down. The left leg is extended strongly from the hip through the knee of the pointed toe. Her head should be turned left to glance at the extended foot. For additional style details, see Tango, pp. 64–65.

LEAD: To lead into a pivot turn clockwise, the man should hold the woman slightly closer, but with sudden body tension. Resistance is exerted outward by both man and woman leaning away from each other in order to take advantage of the centrifugal force of the circular motion. The right foot steps between partner's feet, forward on line of direction, while the left foot reaches across the line of direction and turns on the ball of the foot about three-quarters of the way around. The man must take care not to step too long backward or to dip too low as it is difficult for both man and woman to recover in good style.

NOTE: The exciting part about the corté is that it may be used as a variation in the dance or it may be used as a finishing step at the end of the music. It is perfectly acceptable to end a beat or two in advance and hold the position to the end of the music. It is also acceptable to corté after the music has finished. There is no pressure to get the corté on the last note of the music.

■ *Box Step Series—Westchester*

Westchester Box Step	Cross Step	Grapevine Step
Box Turn	Twinkle Step	

The Westchester box is based on slow quick quick rhythm in 4/4 or cut time. It is a one-measure pattern–but it takes two measures to complete the box–with uneven rhythm, but it is done in a smooth style. It is a combination of dance walk and side close.

▪ WESTCHESTER BOX STEP

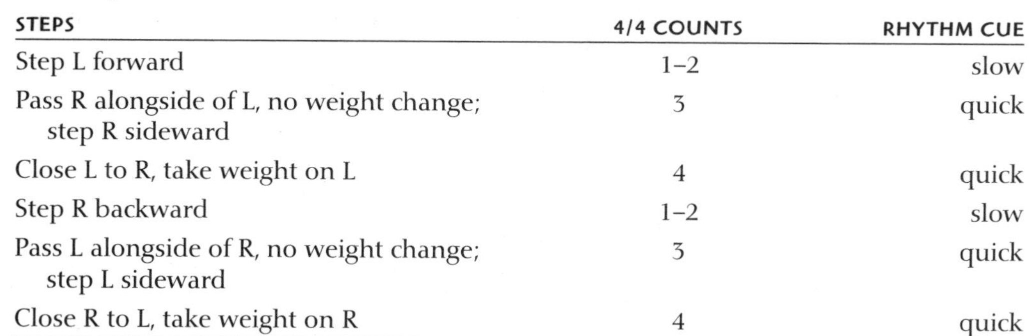

(Closed position)

STEPS	4/4 COUNTS	RHYTHM CUE
Step L forward	1–2	slow
Pass R alongside of L, no weight change; step R sideward	3	quick
Close L to R, take weight on L	4	quick
Step R backward	1–2	slow
Pass L alongside of R, no weight change; step L sideward	3	quick
Close R to L, take weight on R	4	quick

STEP CUE:			
(a)	Forward	side	close.
	S	Q	Q
(b)	Backward	side	close
	long steps	short	steps.

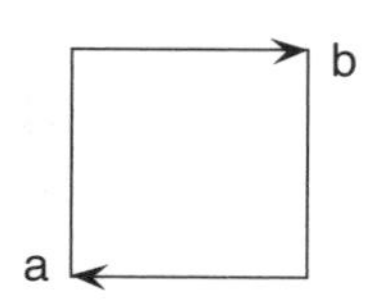

Floor pattern

Fundamental Foxtrot Steps (continued)

STYLE: The forward step is a heel step. Both forward and backward steps should be long reaching steps. Dancers must not lose a beat by pausing as they slide alongside the standing foot.

LEAD: To lead a box step the man should use a forward body action followed by right-hand pressure and right elbow pull to the right to take the woman into the forward sequence of the box. Forward pressure of the right hand followed by pressure to the left side takes the woman into the back sequence of the box.

NOTE: The man must understand the concept of the forward side close as being the forward sequence of the box and the backward side close as being the back sequence of the box. It is important because this terminology will be used in future patterns and leads.

▪ BOX TURN

(Left) (Closed position)

STEPS	4/4 COUNTS	RHYTHM CUE
Step L forward, toe out; turn one-quarter to L	1–2	slow
Step R sideward	3	quick
Close L to R, take weight on L	4	quick
Step R backward, toe in; turn one-quarter to L	1–2	slow
Step L sideward	3	quick
Close R to L, take weight on R	4	quick
Step L forward, toe out; turn one-quarter to L	1–2	slow
Step R sideward	3	quick
Close L to R, take weight on L	4	quick
Step R backward, toe in; turn one-quarter to L	1–2	slow
Step L sideward	3	quick
Close R to L, take weight on R	4	quick

STEP CUE: Turn side close, turn side close.

STYLE: The woman is taking the reverse of this pattern except that, when the woman steps forward with her left foot, instead of toeing out as described for the man, she steps forward between man's feet. This style for the woman greatly facilitates the turn.

LEAD: Refer to lead indications above. A cue for the lead might be bank side close, draw side close.

NOTE: The man may use this turn to maneuver himself into any direction he may wish to use next.

▪ CROSS STEP

(Closed position)

This is a simple but pretty step turning to open dance position momentarily on the forward sequence.

STEPS	4/4 COUNTS	RHYTHM CUE
Step L forward	1–2	slow
Step R sideward, turning to open position	3	quick
Close L to R, take weight on L	4	quick
Step R forward in open position	1–2	slow
Step L forward, turning on L foot to face partner in closed position	3	quick
Close R to L, take weight R	4	quick

STEP CUE: Forward side close, cross side close.

STYLE: The man and woman do not open up to a side to side position but open just enough to step forward on the inside foot, which feels like a crossing step. It should be accented by a long reaching step on the heel but not a dipping knee or body action.

LEAD: To lead into an open position or conversation position, the man should use pressure with the heel of the right hand to turn the woman into open position. The right elbow lowers to the side. The man must simultaneously turn his own body, not just the woman so that they end facing the same direction. The left arm relaxes slightly and the left hand sometimes gives the lead for steps in the open position.

LEAD: To lead from open to closed position, the man should use pressure of the right hand and raise the right arm up to standard position to move the woman into closed position. She should not have to be pushed but should swing easily into closed position as she feels the arm lifting. She should move completely around to face the man squarely.

NOTE: It is possible to go into this step when the man is facing out so that the cross step may travel into the line of direction.

▪ TWINKLE STEP

(Closed position)

This is a slow quick quick rhythm using right and left parallel positions, led from the forward sequence of the box pattern.

STEPS	4/4 COUNTS	RHYTHM CUE
Step L forward	1–2	slow
Step R sideward	3	quick
Close L to R, take weight on L	4	quick
Step R diagonally forward in R parallel position	1–2	slow
Step L sideward, turning from R parallel to L parallel position	3	quick
Close R to L, take weight on R	4	quick
Step L diagonally forward in L parallel position	1–2	slow
Step sideward R, turning from L parallel to R parallel position	3	quick
Close L to R, take weight on L	4	quick
Step R diagonally forward in R parallel position	1–2	slow
Step L sideward turning to closed position	3	quick
Close R to L take weight on R	4	quick

STEP CUE: Slow quick quick.

STYLE: The quick steps are small. Changing from one parallel position to the other is done in a very smooth rolling manner. The woman needs lots of practice alone to learn the back side close pattern because it is on the diagonal backward parallel to the man.

LEAD: To lead into right parallel position the man should not use pressure of his right hand, but rather should raise his right arm rotating the woman counterclockwise one-eighth of a turn while he rotates counterclockwise one-eighth of a turn. This places the man and woman off to the side of each other facing opposite directions. The woman is to the right of the man but slightly in front of him. The man should avoid turning too far so as to be side by side as this results in poor style and awkward and uncomfortable motion. The man's left hand may assist the lead by pulling toward his left shoulder.

Fundamental Foxtrot Steps (continued)

LEAD: To lead from right parallel position to left parallel position, the man should pull with his right hand lowering the right arm and push slightly with his left hand causing a rotation clockwise about a quarter of a turn until the woman is to the left of him but slightly in front of him. They are not side by side.

NOTE: Progress is a zigzag pattern down the floor. The parallel part of the steps may be repeated as many times as desired before going back to closed position.

■ GRAPEVINE STEP

(Closed position)

It is a beautiful pattern in slow quick quick time with four quick steps added to make the grapevine design, using parallel position.

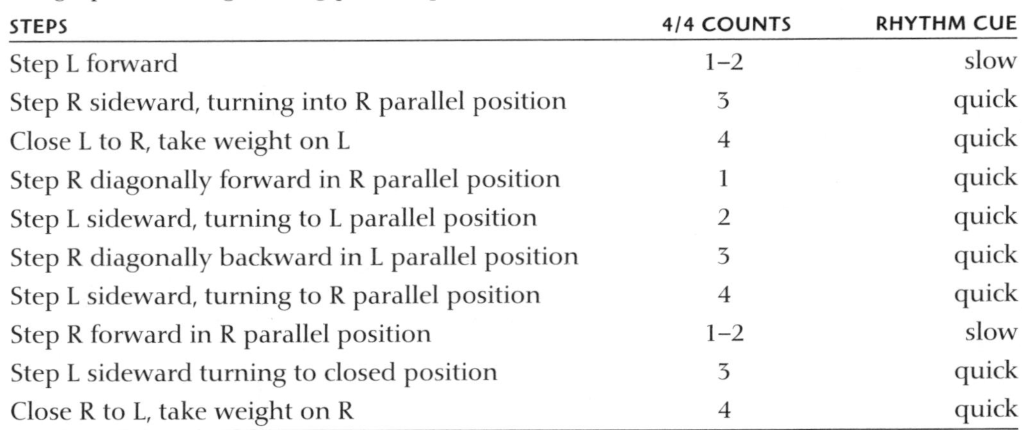

STEPS	4/4 COUNTS	RHYTHM CUE
Step L forward	1–2	slow
Step R sideward, turning into R parallel position	3	quick
Close L to R, take weight on L	4	quick
Step R diagonally forward in R parallel position	1	quick
Step L sideward, turning to L parallel position	2	quick
Step R diagonally backward in L parallel position	3	quick
Step L sideward, turning to R parallel position	4	quick
Step R forward in R parallel position	1–2	slow
Step L sideward turning to closed position	3	quick
Close R to L, take weight on R	4	quick

STEP CUE:

slow quick quick	quick quick quick quick	slow quick quick
forward sequence of box	grapevine pattern	transition back to closed position

STYLE: Practice on the grapevine step alone will help dancers get this pattern smoothly and beautifully. Cue man: forward side back side (R, L, R, L) on the grapevine step. Cue woman: back side forward side (L, R, L, R) on the grapevine step.

LEAD: To lead into right parallel position the man should not use pressure of his right hand, but rather should raise his right arm rotating the woman counterclockwise one-eighth of a turn while he rotates counterclockwise one-eighth of a turn. This places the man and woman off to the side of each other facing opposite directions. The woman is to the right of the man but slightly in front of him. The man should avoid turning too far so as to be side by side as this results in poor style and awkward and uncomfortable motion. The man's left hand may assist the lead by pulling toward his left shoulder.

LEAD: To lead from right parallel position to left parallel position, the man should pull with his right hand lowering the right arm and push slightly with his left hand causing a rotation clockwise about a quarter of a turn until the woman is to the left of him but slightly in front of him. They are not side by side.

LEAD: The lead is from the forward sequence of the box.

NOTE: The man should maneuver so that he is facing out before he starts this step in order that the grapevine step may travel in the line of direction. He may maneuver into this by use of a three-quarter turn or a hesitation step.

■ *The Pivot Turn*

The continuous pivot turn is a series of steps turning clockwise as many beats as desired. The man should be careful that he has room to turn, as the pivot turn progresses forward in the line of direction if done properly, and he should not turn so many steps as to make his partner dizzy. The principle involved in the footwork is the dovetailing of the feet, which means that the right foot always steps between partner's feet and the left foot always steps around the outside of partner's feet. The pivot turn described here has two slow beats as a preparation followed by four quick beats turning and comes out of it into the box step.

▪ THE PIVOT TURN

(Closed position)

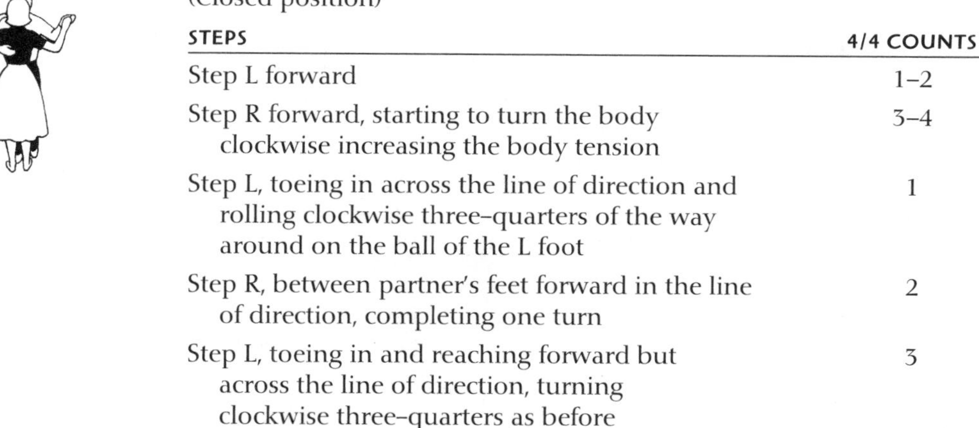

STEPS	4/4 COUNTS	RHYTHM CUE
Step L forward	1–2	slow
Step R forward, starting to turn the body clockwise increasing the body tension	3–4	slow
Step L, toeing in across the line of direction and rolling clockwise three-quarters of the way around on the ball of the L foot	1	quick
Step R, between partner's feet forward in the line of direction, completing one turn	2	quick
Step L, toeing in and reaching forward but across the line of direction, turning clockwise three-quarters as before	3	quick
Step R, between partner's feet forward in the line of direction, completing the second turn	4	quick
Step L forward in the line of direction, not turning but controlling momentum	1–2	slow
Step R sideward	3	quick
Close L to R, take weight on L	4	quick
Step R backward	1–2	slow
Step L sideward	3	quick
Close R to L, taking weight R	4	quick

STEP CUE: Step ready
S S
turn turn turn turn
Q Q Q Q
forward side close
S Q Q
back side close
S Q Q

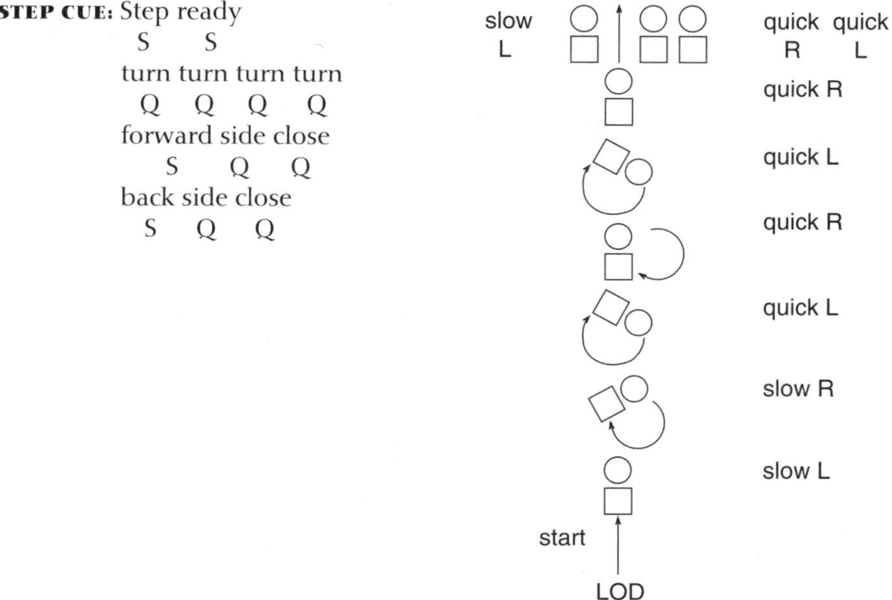

THE WOMAN: On the second slow beat, the woman receives the lead as the man increases body tension. She does the same. Then, on the first quick beat, she has been turned far enough to place her right foot forward in between his feet on the line of direction, left foot across the line of direction, right foot between, left across, and into the box step.

Fundamental Foxtrot Steps (continued)

STYLE: They both must lean away, pressing outward like "the water trying to stay in the bucket." The concept of stepping each time in relation to the line of direction is what makes it possible to progress while turning as a true pivot turn should do.

LEAD: To lead all turns, the man dips his shoulder in the direction of the turn and his upper torso turns before his leg and foot turn.

LEAD: To lead into a pivot turn clockwise, the man should hold the woman slightly closer, but with sudden body tension. Resistance is exerted outward by both man and woman leaning away from each other in order to take advantage of the centrifugal force of the circular motion. The right foot steps between partner's feet, forward on line of direction, while the left foot reaches across the line of direction and turns on the ball of the foot about three-quarters of the way around.

FOXTROT COMBOS

The Foxtrot routines are listed here merely as examples to show how the various steps can be used in combination for practice routines. They are listed from simple to complex. (Closed position, unless otherwise indicated.)

1. *Dance Walk*
   4 dance walk forward
   4 dance walk backward
   4 dance walk forward
   4 dance walk, travel left in a circle
2. *Dance Walk*
   4 dance walk forward
   2 pen magic step
   conversation pivot
3. *Magic Step*
   2 magic steps
   2 open magic steps
   conversation pivot
4. *Magic Step—Box*
   2 magic steps
   1 box step
   2 magic steps (open)
5. *Magic Step/Corté*
   1 magic step (open or closed)
   corté (recover)
   1 side close
   1 box turn
   corté (recover)
6. *Advanced Combo*
   1 magic step
   1 single twinkle to open
   1 single twinkle to left parallel
   1 single twinkle to open
   1 single twinkle to close

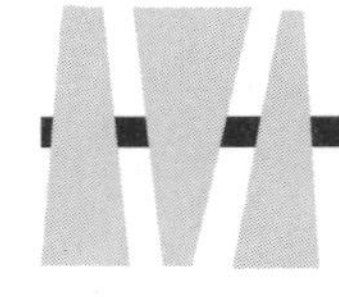

Disco Dance

DISCO STANDS TO the seventies as Rock stood to the sixties. *Disco* comes from the word *discotheque,* which in France is a place where records and disques are stored. In the United States, a discotheque is a place where records are played and one can listen or dance to rock music. Disco Dance has become a descriptive term that encompasses a wide variety of dance steps to many musical rhythms. Originally the partners did not touch and the patterns were simple, characterized by (1) stationary base, (2) response to a steady beat–predominantly 4/4 time, (3) action in the upper torso (this is styling of hands and movement of body above the hips), and (4) not following the lead of a partner.

What began as fury and inspiration became fashion. How to keep the momentum going became a major concern as record sales declined and disco attendance dropped. Two events occurred that increased the desire of the whole nation for dance. Studio 54 in New York City proved that a discotheque could work on a grand scale. People wanted an opportunity to exhibit themselves. Gone were the glitter balls; they were replaced by video screens with computer graphics. The disc jockey continued to be in the driver's seat. The dance floor was more spacious. The music and the atmosphere for overstimulation was shared with a profusion of lights, sound, rhythm, and spectacles that could be interpreted as the formula for "pleasure and high times."

The other event was the movie *Saturday Night Fever.* John Travolta strutted and presented a virile young man's need to be assertive, seeking a stage on which to perform.

"Touch dancing" was the new phrase for holding one's partner. The Hustle is credited with bringing people together again on the dance floor. One of the common tunes for dancing was "Feelings"–the dance included body contact, dancing in one spot, responding to the music, and a 4/4 rhythm.

Clubs reopened and new ones arrived to meet the new disco interest. With the Hustle, partners touching once again, the dance studios were back in business. Many of the old forms, like the Lindy and the Latin Dances, as well as the closed dance position or variations, reappeared. Disco in the '90s refers to dance. The music is rock or a blend of soul, reggae, and disco–an irresistible mix of sounds. The music may be live or recorded.

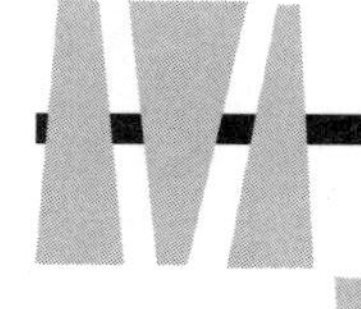

Disco Swing

DISCO SWING FOLLOWS the syncopated rhythm of rock and roll. Many are dancing 4-count swing (even rhythm, Single Lindy) or 6-count swing (uneven rhythm, the Double Lindy). The dance is smoother and glides more like Country Western than Jitterbug. The turns are the same as Swing, but perhaps with different names. The approach to Disco Swing is more casual as the dancers explore one move after another; the feet pause or ignore the step pattern while turns or twirls are in progress; when the maneuvers are completed, the dancers pick up the beat and resume the step pattern. In the discos, with today's social climate and the advent of assertive feminism, it is acceptable for the woman to lead the moves.

Whoever knows the leads, leads. The leads may be pressure from the hands, or eye or verbal contact. Refers to Swing for 6-counts (Double Lindy) pp. 44–45. Follow the directions for the many turns of the Double Lindy.

The Hustle

THE HUSTLE IS WRITTEN in 4/4 time. The accent is on the first beat of each measure. Traditionally the Hustle is danced to 6 counts of music (one and half measures). The tap (touch) step is characteristic of all Hustles.

4/4								
	/				/			
	tap	step	tap	step	step	step		
	Q Q	S	Q Q	S	S	S		
	1	2	3	4	5	6		

CALIFORNIA HUSTLE

There are many Hustles, some for no partners, others for couples. The *California Hustle* is also called the *Los Angeles Hustle* and, in New York, *Bus Stop*.

METER: 4/4. Directions presented in beats.

RECORDS: High/Scope RM9; DC 74528.

CASSETTE: High/Scope RM9.

MUSIC: Betty White Records, How to Hustle D115.

FORMATION: Free formation, all facing music. No partners.

DIRECTIONS FOR THE DANCE

Beats

Starting position: feet together, weight on left.

BACK AND FORWARD STEPS

1–3 Beginning right, take three steps backward.
4 Tap left foot to right foot or point left toe backward. Weight remains on right.
5–7 Beginning left, take three steps forward.
8 Tap right foot to the left foot or point left toe forward. Weight remains on left.
9–12 Repeat steps 1–4.

GRAPEVINE TO SIDE

1 Step left to left side.
2 Step right, crossing in front of left.
3 Step left to left side.
4 Tap right toe to left foot. Weight remains on left.
5 Step right to right side.

6	Step left, crossing in front of right.
7	Step right to right side.
8	Tap left toe to right foot. Weight remains on right.
9–10	Step left to left side; tap right to left–no weight.
11–12	Step right to right side; tap left to right–no weight.

Take a quarter-turn to left to face a new direction and repeat dance.

HUSTLE WITH PARTNER

Directions are for the man; the woman's part is reversed, except when noted.

▪ BASIC STEP

(Closed Position)

STEPS	4/4 COUNTS	RHYTHM CUE
Tap L to side	1	quick
Close L to R, take weight on L	2	quick
Tap R to side	3	quick
Close R to L, take weight on R	4	quick
Step L in place	5	quick
Step R in place	6	quick

STEP CUE: tap step, tap step, step, step.

STYLE: Knees are soft; action should be smooth and rolling rather than bouncy.

▪ TURN

(Clockwise) (Closed position)

STEPS	4/4 COUNTS	STEP CUE
Tap L to side	1	tap
Close L to R, take weight on L	2	step
Tap R to side	3	tap
Step forward right between partner's feet	4	step
Step L forward, turning right (clockwise) pivoting on ball of foot	5	turn
Step R in place, completing turn	6	turn

▪ LINDY

(Closed position)

STEPS	4/4 COUNTS	STEP CUE
Moving into open position step L behind R	1	cross
Step R in place	*and*	step
Moving into closed position, step L to side	2	step
Moving into reverse open position, step R behind L	3	cross
Step L in place	*and*	step
Moving into closed position, step R to side	4	step
Step L in place	5	step
Step R in place	6	step

▪ HUSTLE SWING TURNS

The turns are the same as swing, sometimes with different names. The tap (touch) steps precede the turns, which are made on counts 5, 6. Refer to Double Lindy Variations.

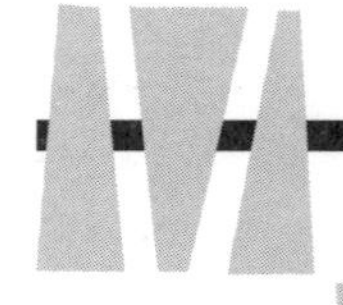

Charleston

THE ROARING TWENTIES saw the advent of Dixieland jazz and the *Charleston.* Definitely a fad dance, the Charleston comes and goes, only to reappear again. The dance, with its fancy footwork and carefree abandon, is a challenge to young and old.

Black dock workers of Charleston, South Carolina, are credited with performing the dance steps eventually referred to as the Charleston. In 1923, the Ziegfeld Follies popularized the step in a show called "Running Wild." Teachers toned the kicking steps down and interspersed them with the Two-Step and Foxtrot, and the United States had a new popular dance. The *Varsity Drag* was one of many dances that incorporated the basic Charleston step. The dance permitted individuals to express their ability with many Charleston variations, independent of their partner.

CHARLESTON RHYTHM

The Charleston rhythm is written in 4/4 time. The bouncy quality of the music occurs in the shift of accent, becoming highly syncopated rhythm.

4/4	/		/		/		/		/
	Q	Q	Q	Q	Q	Q	Q	Q	Q
	&	1	&	2	&	3	&	4	&

The rhythm is an even beat pattern of quicks counted *"and* 1, *and* 2, and *and* 3, *and* 4." The knee bends on the *and* before the step. It is the *and* that gives the Charleston its characteristic bounce. Rhythmically, the beats are:

4/4

The accent shifts from the first beat to the eighth note tied to the third beat, which gives punch to the rhythm. The rhythm is jerky, staccato as well as syncopated.

CHARLESTON STYLE

The twisting of the feet and the bending of the knees before each step, then the straightening of the leg, are basic. The arms move in opposition to the feet: For example, step left, point right and swing both arms across to the left, step right, point left and swing arms across right. The Charleston may be danced as a solo; in a line with a group; or with a partner, side by side, on the same foot, or facing each other, hands joined or closed position.

Charleston with Partner

Partners may be side by side, on the same foot or facing each other, hands joined or closed position. The lead is visual. The man starts with his L, woman R. Any step changes start with man's L. Man and woman stop together.

TEACHING SUGGESTIONS

1. Practice rhythm first. Feet slightly apart and parallel, bend knees (*and*), straighten legs (count 1). Repeat the action of "*and* 1, *and* 2, *and* 3, *and* 4." Then add the music.
2. Practice pivot on balls of feet. Heels out (*and*), heels in (count 1). Repeat.
3. *Charleston Twist.* Combine **1** and **2.** Bend knees and heels out (*and*), straighten legs and heels in (count 1). Repeat.
4. Add arm movement, swinging arms in opposition to feet. Swinging arms helps to maintain balance.
5. If balance and timing are difficult, try sitting on the edge of a chair to establish the rhythm; then stand behind the chair, holding onto the back for support.
6. Teach all figures in place. Then move forward and backward. Practice without music, slowly. If record player has a variable speed, introduce music as soon as possible. Gradually increase tempo until the correct tempo is reached.

FUNDAMENTAL CHARLESTON STEPS

RECORD: "The Golden Age of the Charleston," EMI Records LTD., GX 2507; or any good recording of the 1920s.

FORMATION: Free formation, all facing music.

▪ POINT STEP

(Feet together, weight on R)

STEPS	4/4 COUNTS	DIRECTION CUE
Bend R knee	*and*	*and*
Step forward L	1	step forward
Bend L knee	*and*	*and*
Point R toe forward, straighten knees	2	point forward
Bend L knee	*and*	*and*
Step back R	3	step back
Bend R knee	*and*	*and*
Point L toe back, straighten knees	4	point forward

ARMS: Swing arms in opposition to legs. R toe forward, L arm swings forward, R arm swings back; L toe forward, R arm swings forward, L arm swings back.

▪ SINGLE KICK STEP

(Feet together, weight on R)

STEPS	4/4 COUNTS	DIRECTION CUE
Bend R knee	*and*	*and*
Step forward L	1	step forward
Bend L knee	*and*	*and*
Kick R leg forward, straighten knees	2	kick forward
Bend L knee	*and*	*and*
Step back R	3	step back
Bend R knee	*and*	*and*
Kick L leg back	4	kick back
Straighten knees	*and*	*and*

ARMS: Swing arms in opposition to the kick. Kick R leg forward, L arm swings forward, R arm swings back; kick L leg forward, R arm swings forward, L arm swings back.

Fundamental Charleston Steps (continued)

Variations

1. *Double Kick.* Step forward left; kick right forward, then backward; step right in place. Repeat kicking left forward,then backward; step left.
2. *Single Diagonal Kick.* Step sideward left, kick diagonally forward across left leg, step sideward right, kick diagonally forward across right leg.

THE CHARLESTON TWIST

(Weight on the balls of both feet, heels touching, toes pointing out)

1. The twist comes from pivoting on balls of feet, heels turned out, then pivoting on balls of feet, heels turned in. Heels are slightly off the floor to allow the pivot action.

STEPS	4/4 COUNTS	DIRECTION CUE
Bend knees, pivot in on balls of feet	*and*	heels out
Pivot out, straighten knees	1	heels in
Repeat over and over.		

2. Twist and snap (heels touching, toes pointing out, weight on R).

STEPS	4/4 COUNTS	DIRECTION CUE
Bend R knee, pivot in on ball of foot, lifting L leg up, knee turned in	*and*	heel out
Pivot out on ball of R foot; straighten knees; place L foot by heel of R, toe pointed out; L takes weight	1	heel in
Bend L knee; pivot in on ball of foot, lifting L leg up, knee turned in	*and*	heel out
Pivot out on ball of L foot, straighten knees, place R foot by heel of L, toe pointed out; R takes weight	2	heel in

JUMP

STEPS	4/4 COUNTS	DIRECTION CUE
Bend both knees together	*and*	bend
Jump forward diagonally L, both arms swing L, shoulder height	1	jump
Bend both knees	*and*	bend
Jump back, both arms swing down	2	jump
Repeat jump and arms forward and back	*and* 1 *and* 2	
Bend both knees together	*and*	
Jump forward diagonally R, both arms swing R, shoulder height	1	jump
Bend both knees together	*and*	
Jump back, both arms swing down	2	jump
Repeat jump and arms forward and back	*and* 1 *and* 2	jump jump
Alternately jump L R L R, arms swing L R L R	*and* 1 *and* 2	jump

SWIVEL

Weight on heel, pivot toes R (count *and*); weight on toes, pivot heels R (count 1). Continue to move R, heel, toe, heel, toe. Arms swing L and down, repeating with heel, toe. Travel on counts *and* 1 *and* 2. Reverse movement to travel L.

■ **SUZY Q**

Pivoting on L heel and R toe simultaneously (count *and*), then pivoting on L toe and R heel simultaneously (count 1). Continue alternating, traveling R. Hands in front of chest, elbows out as heels are apart; drop elbows as toes are apart; alternate elbows out and dropped with foot movement. Reverse footwork to travel L.

Twelfth Street Rag

TWELFTH STREET RAG is a novelty dance composed to a popular tune.

RECORDS: DC 74505; High/Scope RM5.

CASSETTES: DC 15X; High/Scope RM5.

FORMATION: Single circle, hands joined; scattered; or lines of four to five, hands joined, facing line of direction.

STEPS: Strut, Charleston, grapevine.

DIRECTIONS FOR THE DANCE

METER: 4/4

■ *Measures*

1	Beginning left, strut four steps forward.
2	Point left toe forward, then to side. Beginning left, take three steps backward.
3–4	Beginning right, repeat action of measures 1–2.
5	Beginning left, take seven quick steps sideward to left. Type of step options could be shuffle, step close, grapevine, and swivel steps.
6	Beginning right, take seven quick steps sideward to right.
7–8	Beginning left, take two Charleston steps in place.
	Repeat dance.

■ **INTERLUDE**

1	Jump forward on both feet, throwing hands up in air. Jump backwards on both feet, throwing hands back, turn and face the other way.
2	Turn individually to own right, taking three steps (strut right, left, right) and clap own hands on fourth count. Improvise during interlude.

Swing (Jitterbug)

SWING IS AN UMBRELLA term for a wide variety of dance, such as West Coast Swing, East Coast Swing, Jive, Jitterbug, Shag, and Lindy Hop. With the advent of Dixieland jazz during the Roaring Twenties, a variety of dances appeared, including the *Lindbergh Hop.* Lindbergh had just completed his successful trans-Atlantic trip, a "hop" over to France. Later the dance was just called the *Lindy.* Cab Calloway is credited to referring to the Lindy hoppers as "jitterbuggers." It went through a fad period of being extremely eccentric with its wild acrobatics inspired by the rising popularity of boogie woogie. The Big Apple, the Shag, and the Lindy were all products of that period. They changed after World War II to a more syncopated rhythm called Rock and Roll with the double Lindy pattern and to the Swing with the smooth, sophisticated triple rhythm, which came in a short time later. All during the Rock period, both Double and Triple Lindy could be seen on American Bandstand. A softer sound called boogie, but no relation to boogie woogie, has greater synthesization of electronic equipment.

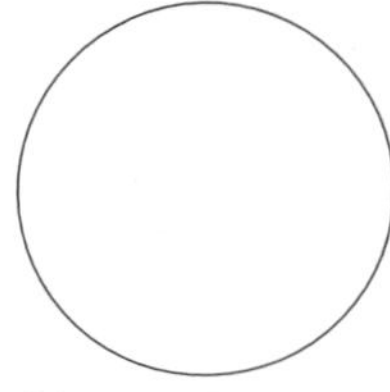

Circular Space for
Swing Dance

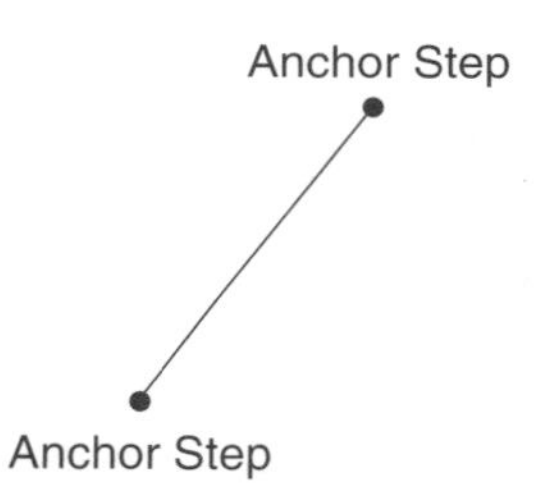

Narrow Space for
West Coast Swing Dance

Swing is danced to a wide variety of music and reflects the dance style of the particular music–Big Band music of the '50s, Rock and Roll, Rhythm, and Blues, Salsa, Reggae, Country Western, and Cajun–all written in 4/4 or cut time. Swing includes the rhythm of Single Lindy, Double Lindy, Triple Lindy. Some refer to these as Jitterbug. The term "Swing" is also applied to myriad of figures as the couple covers a *circular space* in one area. There is wide variation in the footwork and figures.

East Coast Swing and **Triple Lindy** are synonymous. **West Coast Swing** is a more difficult and sophisticated dance. West Coast Swing is referred to as a *slot dance* because the couple moves back and forth in a *narrow* space, always the same space. The dance evolved in the '50s on the West Coast in the small clubs where dance space was limited.

We will continue to use the term *Swing* for Single, Double, and Triple Lindy.

SWING RHYTHM

Swing is written in 4/4 or cut time. It is extremely adaptable to fast or slow rhythm or to 4/4 time from Foxtrot to hard rock in quality. The Shag was actually the first dance to be called Jitterbug, and its slow slow quick quick rhythm set the pattern for all of the others. The Single Lindy has the same rhythm. It is done occasionally by older adults because of the slower pace it sets, but was not really in use much in the 1980s. It is shown here to demonstrate the transition into the more active Swing patterns.

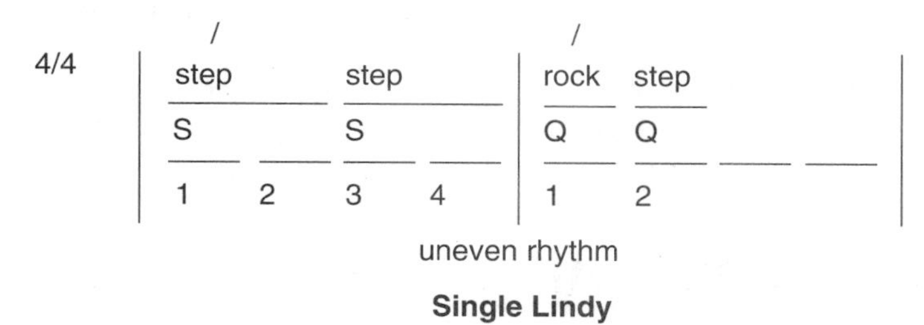

Single Lindy

The Double Lindy is very adaptable to slow or fast music and is the rhythm that is coming back as the new Jitterbug. Accent is on the offbeat.

4/4		/		/		/
	dig	step	dig	step	rock	step
	Q	Q	Q	Q	Q	Q
	1	2	3	4	1	2

even rhythm

Double Lindy

The Triple Lindy is more often danced to the slow, mellow, sophisticated tempos.

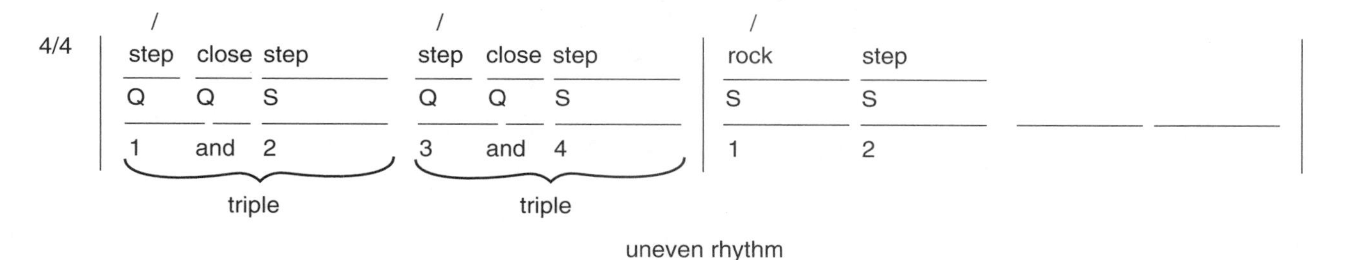

Triple Lindy—East Coast Swing

SWING STYLE

Exciting styles and positions are in use for Swing. It is a matter of taste for the individual dancers whether they use a dig step, a step-hop, or a kick step. However, the basic rhythm must be maintained by both man and woman in order to coordinate the pattern together, unlike Discotheque, in which the step or rhythm pattern of each partner is unstructured. The man is able to lead the dance because of the magnificent body alertness of both partners. A firm body and a calculated resistance in the arm and fingers enable quick response in any direction. The space between partners is controlled by a spring tension in the elbow, which never extends fully but allows the pull away and the spring back smoothly and with control. The woman uses her arm as a pivot center. The elbow is down and the hand is up for the underarm turns, and she turns around her arm but does not let it fly in the air. There should never be the appearance of arms flying loose or entangled. The fingers slip easily around one another without losing contact. Even the free arm is bent and remains close to the body.

Swing (continued)

Swing steps tend to cover a circular space in one area of the floor. The footwork is at all times small and close together, with rolling and turning on the ball of the foot. The turning action for beginner steps is always on the first step (count 2) of the pattern when the woman is on her right foot and the man is on his left. The rhythm pattern is generally the same over and over but the changes of position and direction and the constant subtle smooth roll to offbeat rhythm generates a fabulous excitement for both dancer and observer.

WEST COAST SWING RHYTHM

West Coast Swing Rhythm is 6 or 8 beats. It is a slower rhythm than East Coast Swing.

All Uneven Rhythm

4/4

anchor step

step step touch step step step step

S S S S Q Q S

1 2 3 4 1 & 2

1 2 3 4 5 & 6

triple

uneven rhythm—6 count

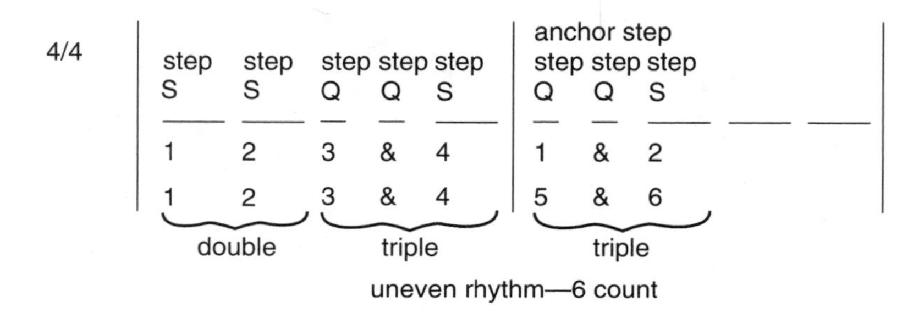

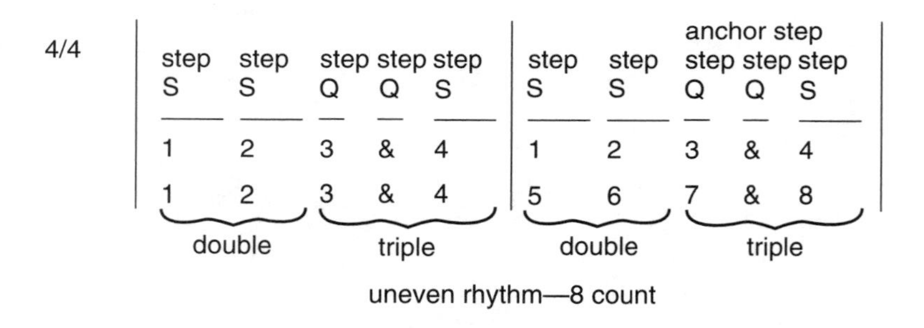

WEST COAST SWING STYLE

The woman's step is different than the man's; partners do not mirror each other. The step is like the Cuban walk (p. 118). Little kicks and toe touches on the beat give flair for a sophisticated look. The anchor steps (quick, quick, slow) occur at the end of the slot. The couples move in a narrow space.

FUNDAMENTAL SWING STEPS

Directions are for the man; the woman's part is reversed, except when noted.

The Double Lindy

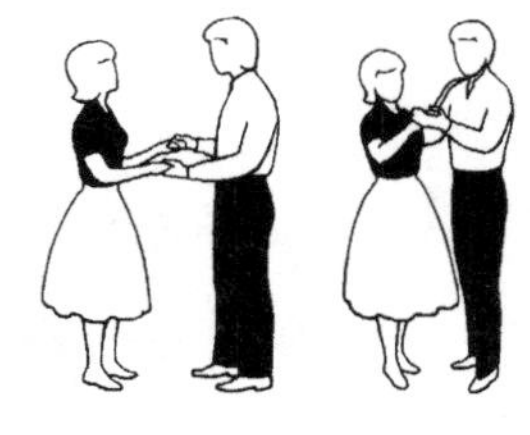

(Beginners–Two hands joined; experienced–Semiopen position)

STEPS	4/4 COUNTS	RHYTHM CUE
Touch L to instep of R	1	quick
Step L in place	2	quick
Touch R to instep of L	3	quick
Step R in place	4	quick
Step L backward, a little behind R heel	1	quick
Step R forward	2	quick

STEP CUE: Dig step, dig step, rock step.

STYLE: The body takes a *slight* motion, tipping forward from the waist and dipping the outside shoulder (man's L, woman's R) on the first dig step like an upbeat. Take care not to exaggerate this motion. It is very subtle. The dig is a touching of the toe lightly to the instep of the other foot. It should not be a tap step that makes noise on the floor. The feet are close together for this beat. The weight is carried on the ball of the foot and the steps are small throughout the step. The amount of knee bend depends on individual preference as to style; however, the action should be smooth and rolling rather than bouncy.

NOTE: Beginners must learn this pattern alone until they can move accurately with the rhythm. Then dancers take two hands joined, man's hands palm up. The elbow is down, forearm is firm, and fingers exert resistance against partner's. On the rock step there is a spring tension in the arms that allows an "apart–together" action that is smooth and has arm control.

LEAD: The man holds both of their hands close together and dips slightly with his left shoulder on the first dig step. The woman pushes slightly against his hands on the first dig step so as to receive his lead. This technique teaches the woman to give the necessary resistance for all future leads.

NOTE: The above progression provides instant success with Swing. The variations listed are arranged in the order recommended. In describing the variations, the analysis will refer to action on the first dig, the first step, the second dig, the second step, the rock step or the first dig step, second dig step, or the entire pattern, rather than by counts as in other dances.

Double Lindy Variations

Collegiate
Break to Semiopen Position
Semiopen Basic
Basic Turn
Swing Out Break
Continuous Underarm Turns
Brush Off
Tuck Spin
Wrap
Double Brush Off
Dish Rag
Overhead Swing

Fundamental Swing Steps (continued)

▪ COLLEGIATE

(Two hands joined, man's hands palm up)

STEPS	STEP CUE
Man brings both hands close together and dips the left shoulder	first dig
Man steps L forward close to the L of the woman, pivots clockwise at close range on the L foot	first step
Woman steps R diagonally forward across to the R of the man at close range and pivots clockwise on the R foot	first step
Both take dig and step in place	second dig step
Both rock out and in using arm control	rock step

STEP CUE: Dig turn, dig in place, rock step.

STYLE: Resistance in the arms and fingers hold the couple in a tight, close-facing position on the pivot turn. Each needs to step in close to partner on the pivot foot (man's L, woman's R). The steps are small.

LEAD: The man can help the woman pivot by the pull of his hands and body. He dips the left shoulder on the first dig to give her the cue for this turn. When used in combination with other variations, the man will take or release hands on the rock steps. (a) An optional lead is to reach sideways with each hand shoulder high on the first step and bring the hands back together on the second step. This creates a butterfly turn effect. (b) A second optional and more advanced lead is the man may pivot to right parallel position on the first dig and to left parallel on the first step. It is a quick change of position like a cock turn and is led by a push and pull action in the hands. The second dig step and rock step are the same as before.

▪ BREAK TO SEMIOPEN POSITION

(Two hands joined)

STEPS	STEP CUE
Dig in place, the man preparing to pull the woman toward him	first dig
Man and woman step toward each other, the man pulling the L hand downward and placing R arm around her waist	first step
Both take dig step, pivoting to semiopen position	second dig
Both step backward a short step in semiopen position	second step
Rock step in same position	rock step

STEP CUE: Pull down, come together, rock step.

STYLE: The steps are small.

LEAD: The man pulls down on her hand so that, as they come into semiopen position, the man's left hand holding the woman's right hand ends up in the correct position for basic.

▪ SEMIOPEN BASIC

(Semiopen position)

STEPS	STEP CUE
Dig in place, L to instep of R	first dig
Step forward a short step L	first step
Dig R to instep of L	second dig
Step backward a short step R	second step
Rock step	rock step

STEP CUE: Dig step, dig step, rock step.

STYLE: Dancers remain in semiopen position throughout. All steps are small close to the body. The man's fingers reach around the little-finger side of the woman's hand.

■ BASIC TURN

(Semiopen position)

The basic turn is used in semiopen position as previously described. When repeated over and over, it should be done turning the couple around in place clockwise. The man makes the step turn by taking the first step with his left foot on a clockwise curve toward the woman and pivoting about a quarter-turn on the ball of the left foot. He finishes the remainder of the pattern from that new direction. Repeat as desired. As the dancers become skillful at this turn they will find they can turn a half-turn or more each time by pivoting a greater degree on the stepping beat.

STEP CUE: Dig turn, dig-step, rock step.

STYLE: The woman will have no trouble adjusting to this turning action. She will roll on the ball of her foot.

LEAD: A dip of the man's left shoulder and a slight pull of his right arm around her waist take her along easily into the turn.

■ SWING OUT BREAK

(Semiopen position)

The man takes the entire pattern in place once as he turns the woman out under his left arm to face him.

STEPS	STEP CUE
Man moves his L hand from the low position to a position in close at waist level	first dig
Man raises his L hand above her head and turns her under to face him. Woman on R foot pivots clockwise halfway around to face him	first step
Both take a dig step in place facing partner	second dig step
Both rock away and together using elbow control	rock step

STEP CUE: Dig turn, dig step, rock step.

STYLE: Woman keeps the R elbow level with shoulder and forearm at right angles, and turns around her own arm, not under it. His arm is high enough so that she does not have to duck to get under. The woman's pivot step is short so that they do not get too far apart. They must have room to take the rock step with elbow control.

LEAD: The man leads the starting motion by bending his left elbow to bring his hand in to waist level on the first dig. This cues the woman. She is waiting with her right foot in dig position and with the lead she can step with him into the first step. His arm must be raised high enough on the first step to clear her head as she turns under.

NOTE: The face-to-face position is called swing out position–dancers will have one hand joined (man's L, woman's R). The man should bring her back to position by using the break to semiopen position.

■ CONTINUOUS UNDERARM TURNS

(Swing out position)

The man and woman exchange places as he turns her counterclockwise across to his position and steps around her to her position.

STEPS	STEP CUE
Man increases pressure on woman's hand	first dig
Both man and woman take a short step forward. Man turns clockwise on his L foot while turning woman under counterclockwise on her R foot	first step
Take dig and step in place	second dig step
Rock step out and in, controlling with firm arm	rock step

Fundamental Swing Steps (continued)

STEP CUE: Dig turn, dig step, rock step.

STYLE: Both turn halfway around on the first step but stay in close so that there is room for the remainder of the basic step. They have exactly exchanged places after one complete pattern.

LEAD: The man turns his hand knuckles up, fingers down, so that the woman's fingers can slip around his fingers as she turns. Then he brings his hand down palm up.

NOTE: This underarm turn can be repeated over and over. It will serve as a connecting step to any other variation. The man may lead back to semiopen basic or reach for the woman's other hand for any of the two hands joined variations that follow.

▪ BRUSH OFF

(Also called flirtation pass) (Swing out position)

This step begins with the woman in swing out position after one underarm turn, leaving the man's hand in palm-up position. It is basically a man's left turn.

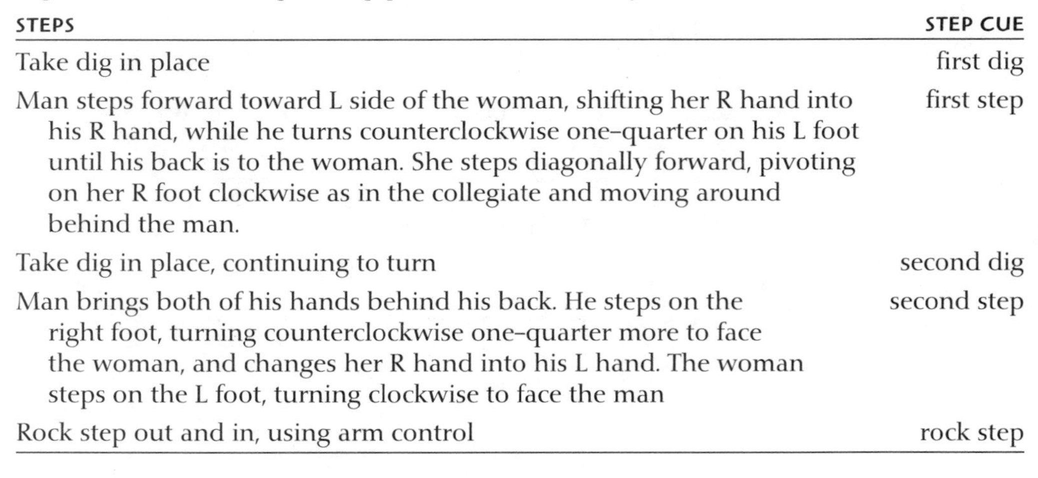

STEPS	STEP CUE
Take dig in place	first dig
Man steps forward toward L side of the woman, shifting her R hand into his R hand, while he turns counterclockwise one-quarter on his L foot until his back is to the woman. She steps diagonally forward, pivoting on her R foot clockwise as in the collegiate and moving around behind the man.	first step
Take dig in place, continuing to turn	second dig
Man brings both of his hands behind his back. He steps on the right foot, turning counterclockwise one-quarter more to face the woman, and changes her R hand into his L hand. The woman steps on the L foot, turning clockwise to face the man	second step
Rock step out and in, using arm control	rock step

STEP CUE: Man turns and turns rock step.

STYLE: While doing this pattern, the couple have exchanged places, each turning a half-turn. The woman can control the space factor because she can stay in close to him as she goes around him.

LEAD: The transfer of hands should be done smoothly and without losing contact.

NOTE: It is especially fun to follow the brush off with an underarm turn. The man should be prepared to lead into it immediately after the rock step.

▪ TUCK SPIN

(Swing out position)

STEPS	STEP CUE
Man moves both of woman's hands to his R (woman turns slightly to her L), pulls woman toward himself in a sharp action	first dig
Man steps in place, releasing her hands; he pushes her in the opposite direction with a quick flip, spinning her clockwise once around on her R foot	first step
Woman catches her balance with the digging foot, man resumes joined-hand position	second dig
They step in place together	second step
Rock step out and in	rock step

STEP CUE: Tuck spin, dig step, rock step.

STYLE: The woman must spin smoothly a full-turn around in place on right foot without losing her balance.

LEAD: There must be firm arm and finger control in order for the woman to respond to this with the proper timing. Woman offers arm resistance. Man catches her left hand in his left, then changes to swing out position.

NOTE: The man may also spin at the same time. His turn will go counterclockwise on the left foot.

▪ WRAP

(Two hands joined)

STEPS	STEP CUE
Take dig, man lifts his L arm and prepares to turn the woman counterclockwise	first dig
Step forward a short step, and, without releasing hands, the man will move his raised L hand across in front of her and up over her head as she is turning counterclockwise one-quarter on her R foot	first step
Dig in place still turning.	second dig
Step backward, as the woman finishes in a position close to him on his R side. His R arm is around her waist and her arms are crossed in front as they finish in the wrap position (his R joins her L)	second step
Rock step back and forward together	rock step

STYLE: A smooth roll is important.

NOTE: To unwrap, the man initiates a reverse roll, turning the woman clockwise back to starting position and assisting with a gentle right-arm push. Another variation on the unwrap is for the man to release with his left hand and pull with the right hand, rolling the woman out to his right. Again this should be taken on the two dig steps and they finish off with the rock in face-to-face position.

▪ DOUBLE BRUSH OFF

(Swing out position)

The couple must know how to do a single brush-off step. The double brush-off step is twice through the rhythm pattern. Starting position is swing out position (man's L, woman's R hand joined).

First time through the rhythm pattern (dig step, dig step, rock step):

STEPS	STEP CUE
Man starts first brush-off step, turning L one-half, woman steps forward slightly	first dig step
He reaches out palm up with his L hand to take her L hand, they are side by side, the woman on the L; the woman's step is in place	second dig step
The man releases her R hand behind his back and reaches around in front under their L hand to take her R hand	rock step

Second time through the rhythm pattern (dig step, dig step, rock step):

STEPS	STEP CUE
Man raises L hand, pulling the woman under with the R and turning her counterclockwise as both hands go up over her head	first dig step
He releases the L hand, as he begins to turn his second brush off, turning counterclockwise as his R arm comes down behind his back	second dig step
He changes her R hand into his L as he finishes his turn to face the woman	rock step

Fundamental Swing Steps (continued)

STYLE: This must have the look of a complete flowing action. The woman must stay in close to the man. Both must keep the dig step, dig step, rock step pattern going in their feet. Steps are small.

LEAD: The most important lead is when the man reaches out palm up to take her left hand. The second lead is when he pulls with the right hand and both hands go over her head.

▪ DISH RAG

(Two hands joined)

The couple rolls to the man's left, woman's right, turning back to back and rolling on around face to face. They must keep the footwork of the Double Lindy going. It is one complete pattern.

▪ OVERHEAD SWING

(Two hands joined)

The couple steps forward right side to right side. Each swings the right arm over partner's head, behind the neck and slides the right hand down the right arm of partner to a right-hand grasp. The dancers must keep the basic footwork going. It is one complete pattern.

The Triple Lindy—East Coast Swing

THE *TRIPLE LINDY* is lovely and pleasant to do to a nice swingy Foxtrot. It should be smooth and relaxing.

▪ TRIPLE RHYTHM

(Semiopen position) (Three little steps to each slow beat; these are similar to a fast Two-Step.)

STEPS	4/4 COUNTS	RHYTHM CUE
Step L forward Close R to L, take weight R Step L forward	1 *and* 2	quick quick slow
Step R backward Close L to R, take weight L Step R backward	3 *and* 4	quick quick slow

Rock Step		
Step L backward, a little behind R heel	1	slow
Step R in place	2	slow

STEP CUE: Shuffle step, shuffle step, rock step.

STYLE: The triple rhythm should be small shuffling steps, keeping the feet close to the floor. Weight is on the ball of the foot. Basic style is that of Double Lindy.

LEAD: The man cues the woman for the triple steps by increasing the tension in his right hand as he starts the shuffle step forward. Other leads are the same as for the Double Lindy.

NOTE: Any of the variations for Double Lindy can be done in triple rhythm, and dancers frequently change from one rhythm to another during one piece of music.

▪ TRIPLE LINDY SWIVEL STEP

(Semiopen position and traveling in line of direction, forward; rhythm pattern changes)

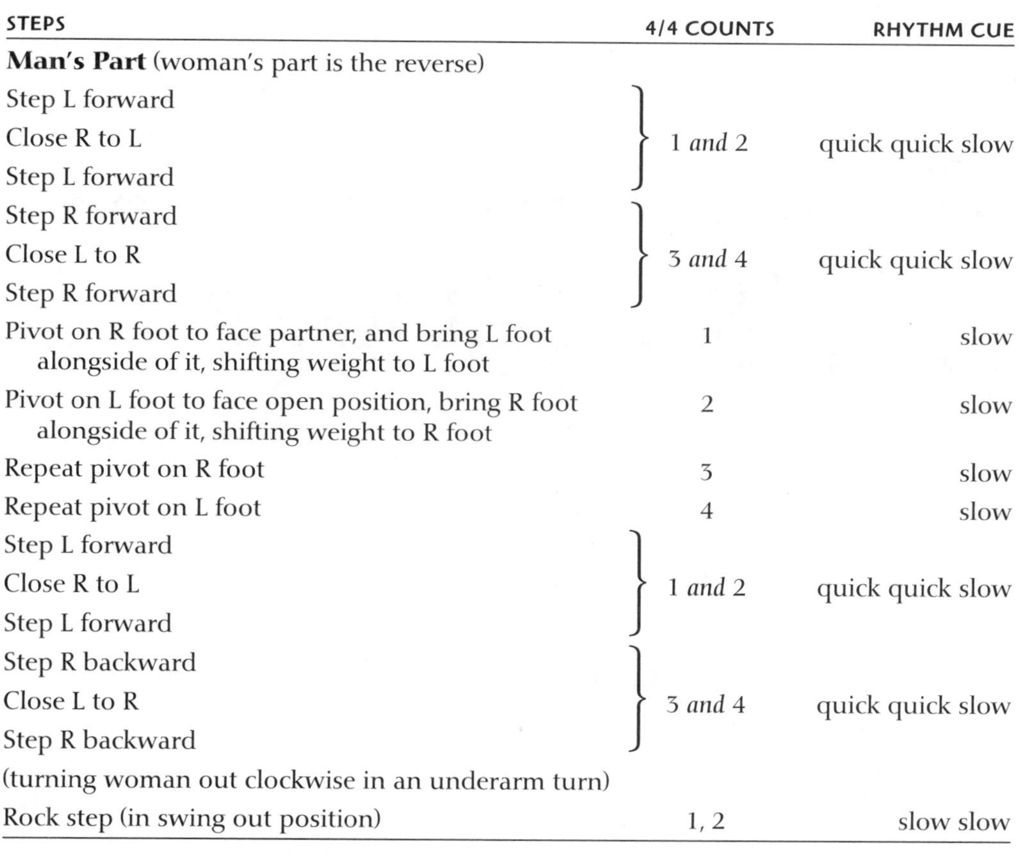

STEPS	4/4 COUNTS	RHYTHM CUE
Man's Part (woman's part is the reverse)		
Step L forward Close R to L Step L forward	1 *and* 2	quick quick slow
Step R forward Close L to R Step R forward	3 *and* 4	quick quick slow
Pivot on R foot to face partner, and bring L foot alongside of it, shifting weight to L foot	1	slow
Pivot on L foot to face open position, bring R foot alongside of it, shifting weight to R foot	2	slow
Repeat pivot on R foot	3	slow
Repeat pivot on L foot	4	slow
Step L forward Close R to L Step L forward	1 *and* 2	quick quick slow
Step R backward Close L to R Step R backward	3 *and* 4	quick quick slow
(turning woman out clockwise in an underarm turn)		
Rock step (in swing out position)	1, 2	slow slow

STEP CUE: Triple step, triple step
swivel 2 3 4
triple step, triple step, rock step.

STYLE: The swivel steps are tiny, crisp, and neatly turning, just a quarter turn on each pivot. The body turns with the foot closed, open, closed, open.

LEAD: The man must lead the swivel step by turning the woman from open to closed, and so forth.

NOTE: The couple progresses along the line of direction as the pivot turn is being done in four quick steps.

The Triple Lindy—East Coast Swing (continued)

SWING COMBOS

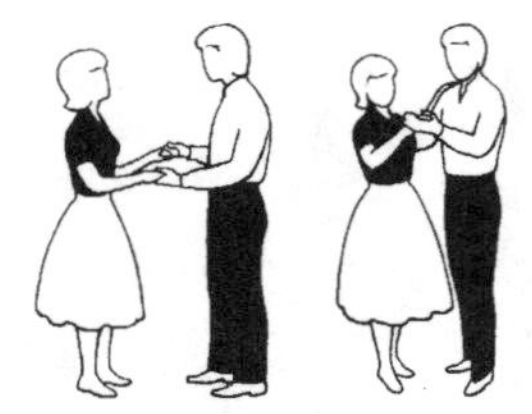

The Swing routines are combinations for practice, which are listed from simple to complex. They may be used for either Shag, Single Lindy, Double Lindy, or Triple Lindy. (Two hands joined or semiopen position, unless otherwise indicated.)

1. *Basic Swing Out and Close*
   1 basic
   single underarm break
   break to original position
2. *Basic–Swing Out–Underarm Turn Close*
   1 basic
   single underarm break
   break to original position
3. *Swing Out and Collegiate*
   2 basics
   single underarm break
   3 collegiate steps
   underarm turn
   original position
4. *Swing Out and Brush Off*
   2 basics
   single underarm break
   brush off
   underarm turn
   original position
5. *Collegiate–Brush Off*
   2 basic
   single underarm break
   underarm turn
   3 collegiate steps
   underarm turn
   brush off
   underarm turn
   original position
6. *Collegiate–Tuck–Spin*
   2 collegiate steps
   tuck spin
   underarm turn
7. *Collegiate–Wrap*
   2 collegiate steps
   wrap
   unwrap
8. *Wrap–Unwrap Spin*
   2 collegiate steps
   wrap
   unwrap
   tuck spin
   underarm turn

West Coast Swing

REFER TO *WEST COAST SWING* definition, diagram, West Coast Rhythm, and West Coast Swing Style page 44.

■ SUGAR PUSH

(Basic step) (Two hands joined)

STEPS	COUNTS	STEP CUE
Man's Part		
Step back L	1	Step
Step R to L	2	Together
Touch L	3	Touch
Step forward L	4	Step
Step R behind L (hook) in place and release man's R, woman's L hand (swing out position)	5	Hook
Step L in place, pushing off	*and*	Step
Step R in place	6	Step
Woman's Part		
Step forward R	1	Step
Step forward L	2	step

Touch R to L instep	3	Touch
Turning R towards partner, step back R (continue to travel in slot)	4	Step
Step L behind R (hook) and release woman's L, man's R hand	5	Hook
Step R in place	*and*	Step
Step L in place	6	Step

STEP CUE: The cue "walk" may be used for counts 1, 2, 4.

STYLE: The footwork and hips are like the Cuban walk (refer to p. 118). Dig, pressing the foot into the floor while moving forward.

LEAD: The arms need to be firm (give weight) as the woman moves forward, the man pulling toward him. On count 3 the woman leans a little more forward, body rising to receive the *push.* On count 4 the man *pushes* as the woman moves backward. Both dancers must offer resistance. The main initiates the *pull* and *push.*

NOTE: The steps on counts 5 and 6 are the "anchor steps." The woman may choose to do a "coaster step" for counts 5 and 6. Coaster step is step back L, close R to L, step forward L.

VARIATION: Triple step. Counts 3, 4 become "3 and 4" (QQS). Instead of Touch Step, man steps LRL, woman steps RLR.

▪ UNDERARM TURN

(Swing out position)

Woman passes the man's R side, turns under her arm to face opposite direction.

STEPS	COUNTS	STEP CUE
Man's Part		
Moving to L side, step L	1	Step
Step forward R	2	Step
Moving toward slot, step L, pivoting clockwise	3	Side
Step R, still turning	*and*	Step
Raising L arm, step L into the slot. Now facing opposite direction	4	Step
Step R behind L	5	Hook
Step L	*and*	Step
Step R in place	6	Step
Woman's Part		
Step forward R	1	Step
Step forward L	2	Step
Take 3 running steps (R, L, R) to the end of slot, turning counterclockwise under R arm, on count 4	3 *and* 4	Run, run, turn
Step L behind R	5	Hook
Step R	*and*	Step
Step L in place	6	Step

LEAD: Man pulls the woman forward, left hand down, raises arm for turn on count 4.

NOTE: Alternate one Sugar Push sequence with one Underarm Turn. Woman may use "coaster step" for counts 5 and 6.

West Coast Swing (continued)

▪ LEFT SIDE PASS

(Swing out position)

Woman passes man's left side.

STEPS	COUNTS	STEP CUE
Man's Part		
Moving to R side, step L across R	1	Step
Pivoting counterclockwise on L, step R near L (now facing slot)	2	Step
Following woman, take 3 steps (L, R, L)	3 *and* 4	Step, step, step
Facing opposite direction, step R behind L	5	Hook
Step L	*and*	Step
Step R in place	6	Step
Woman's Part		
Step forward R	1	Step
Step forward L	2	Step
Passing partner (man's left side), traveling in the slot, take 3 short running steps (R, L, R) pivoting counterclockwise on last run	3 *and* 4	Run, run, turn
Facing opposite direction, step L behind R	5	Hook
Step R	*and*	Step
Step L	6	Step

NOTE: The Left Side Pass is usually preceded by one Sugar Push.

STYLE: Woman holds L arm, elbow bent, to chest as she passes partner and turns.

LEAD: On count 4 man drops L shoulder, pulls his L hand down as woman passes.

▪ WHIP

(Swing out position)

Starting in Swing out position, couple moves into closed position, makes one complete turn clockwise as a couple at the center of the slot, separates into Swing out position, and ends in original position.

STEPS	COUNTS	STEP CUE
Man's Part		
Step back L	1	Step
Moving to L side, step R across L and move into closed position	2	Cross
Step L forward, pivoting clockwise as a couple	3	Turn
Continuing to turn, step R in place	*and*	And
Step L across slot (L and R feet straddle slot)	4	Step
Step R behind L (hook), continuing to turn as a couple	5	Hook
Releasing man's R, woman's L hand and separating, step L forward into slot. Now facing original direction	6	Step
Step R behind L, step L, step R in place	7 *and* 8	Hook, step, step
Woman's Part		
Step forward R toward partner	1	Step
Moving into closed position step L pivoting clockwise to face partner	2	Pivot

Step back R	3	Back
Close L to R	*and*	Together
Step R forward between the man's two feet	4	Step
Continuing to turn clockwise as a couple, step L	5	Step
Release woman's L, man's R hand and step back R	6	Step
Step L behind R, step R, step L in place	7 *and* 8	Hook, step, step

NOTE: Woman's Part, counts 3 and 4, is a *coaster step.* It may be cued as "coaster step" (3 and 4) (QQS).

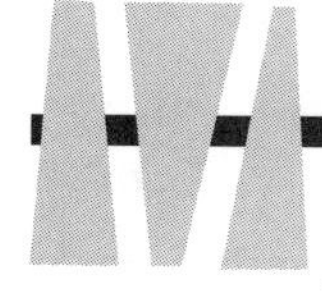

Cajun Dance

CAJUN DANCE, MUSIC, and food are very popular. In the 1980s Chef Paul Prudhomme of New Orleans attracted nationwide attention with his Cajun cooking and references to Cajun culture. Cajun culture suddenly bounced all over the United States. It exemplifies a true spirit of *joie de vivre.* The Cajun heritage is keyed to family, music, and the French language.

The word "Cajun" evolved from the word "Acadian" with the loss of an unstressed syllable (*cf.* Injun from Indian). The Acadians originally came from the French provinces of Normandy and Picardy along the English Channel. The first French colony, Acadie,* was established in 1604 in Nova Scotia, Canada. For political reasons the British deported the Acadians in 1755. Some migrated south, finally settling in the flatlands and bayous of Louisiana with other French. This coastal area, actually 22 of the 64 parishes of Louisiana, is referred to as Acadia, Acadiana, or Evangeline country.

From France the Acadians brought their 17th–18th century culture to the New World. Their culture evolved and adapted with that of the French, English, Spanish, and Afro-Americans. The white French-speaking people of Acadia are referred to as Cajuns; the black French-speaking people are Creoles. (These are not the same Creoles that settled New Orleans.)

Families have always gathered together for social occasions, first at homes and later at barns and dance halls. Music, French ballads, dancing, cards, and of course food were enjoyed. These gatherings were called *fais-dodo* ("go to sleep") because the children were bedded down in another room while the parties lasted till the wee hours. When the halls became night clubs, the children were excluded.

Music

Originally the fiddle was the primary instrument and someone sang old French ballads. The interaction of the Acadians and Creoles influenced the music. The singing became less important as two fiddles played, one melody, one rhythmic backup. More French songs were lost in the 1880s when the German immigrants introduced the button accordion. By the 1920s, the accordion had displaced the fiddles. But during the '30s and '40s fiddles returned as the Cajun musicians were influenced by

*Acadie, which the French called their settlement, was a descriptive word of the Micmac Indians, members of the Algonquin tribe.

Cajun Dance (continued)

their Texas neighbors' Country Western music. Later Bob Wills's western swing, Nashville Country Western music, and rock and roll all touched Cajun music too. After World War II Cajuns returned home with a sense of pride and a rebirth of Cajun music took place. The folk festivals also encouraged traditional Cajun musicians to come forward. Michael Doucet is to be credited with his leadership in restoring interest in traditional Cajun music, encouraging acoustic playing, and playing outside the lounges.

Today the button accordion is the lead instrument and the accordion player also sings French songs. The fiddle and small triangle make up the band. In larger bands there are guitars, spoons, drums, bass, and sometimes brass. Of course there is electric amplification. Cajun music, sometimes referred to as "Chanky Chank" sounds, is a mix of sounds, styles, and cultural history.

A relatively new offshoot of Cajun music is *Zydeco,* a combination of Cajun and rhythm and blues with a Caribbean musical pulse. Eighty years ago a song was written, "Zydeco es Pas Salee," which means "the snap beans have no salt." Zydeco is Cajun slang for the French words "Les Haricots" which means "green snap beans." Today Zydeco means snappy music. Bands include a piano, accordion, and a rubboard (metal washboard or steel vest) strapped on the musicians who wear metal casings on the fingers to produce a myriad of sounds. The songs are in English or French. The rhythm is 4/4 with a strong 1–2, 1–2 beat.

■ Records

Cajun: *Parlez Nous á Boire* (Two-step, swing, blues, waltz), CD 322; *Allon á Lafayette, Bayou Boogie,* Beausoleil; *Stir Up the Roux,* Bruce Daigrepont. Zydeco: *Louisiana Blues and Zydeco,* Clifton Chenier, CD 329; *Louisiana Zydeco Music,* Boo Zoo Chavis. *Motordude Zydeco,* A-2 Fay Records; *Pick Up On This,* CD 2129 and *My Name is Beau Jocque,* Beau Jocque, PCD-1031.

■ Dance

The Acadian dance repertoire included the quadrille, lancer, polka, mazurka, play party types referred to as *Danserond,* and contredanse. Many dances were performed without instrumentation during the 40 days before Lent, so they sang in French, which helped to keep the language alive. Young and old danced, especially those of a "marrying age." The contredanse was more like the Appalachian Big Circle–a country dance. In the late '40s the Cajun round dance scene was very similar to that in Texas. It is almost a step back in time to watch the Cajuns dance the waltz, two-step, one-step. Jitterbug is danced to two-step music. Zydeco is the latest dance. There are two-steps, one-steps, and a few waltzes. Zydeco and Cajun music affect the dancing styles. Cajun dance is smoother, more precise. Dancers circle the floor with more turns and the movement is horizontal. Zydeco dancers move in one spot with greater hip action. The syncopated Zydeco beat generates a bouncy vertical style with few turns. The dancers move subtly, upright with bent knees and lower to the floor. The dance is flavored with small kicks.

Cajun Waltz

METER: 3/4. Directions are for man; woman's part reverse.

FORWARD WALTZ: Closed position. The man pulls the woman close, wrapping most of his right forearm around the woman's shoulder blades. Moving in the line of direction, step on each beat (left, right, left). The first step is longer, followed by a shuffle, shuffle. The man travels forward, woman backward, most of the time; minimal turning. Two measures (6 steps) to turn in place counterclockwise; may turn clockwise.

WOMAN'S TURN: Couple travels forward. Man releases right hand and steps slightly to left side (count 1) and forward (count 2, 3) as woman turns clockwise under his left arm, 3 steps. As she turns, she places her left bent arm behind her back. As she completes the turn the couple resumes the closed position.

DOUBLE TURN: Couple travels forward and man releases right hand. Man takes three steps forward as woman turns with three steps clockwise under his left arm, places her left arm behind her back; woman continues to travel backward as the man turns counterclockwise three steps under his left arm; resumes the closed position.

STYLE: The dance is smooth as if gliding on ice. A fluid movement is achieved by dancing on the balls of the feet and absorbing the movement with bent knees.

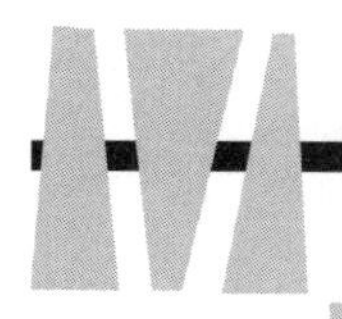

Cajun Two-Step

METER: 2/4 OR 4/4. Directions are for man; woman's part reverse.

Closed position. The man pulls the woman close, wrapping most of his right forearm around the woman's shoulder blades. Progressing forward, the couple turns slowly counterclockwise, strep-close-step touch. Step to the left side, and slightly forward, close right to left, step left in place, touch right to left instep (4 counts). May turn clockwise.

STYLE: The dance is smooth. In some areas, dancers rock slightly side to side.

Cajun One-Step

METER: 4/4. Directions are for man; woman's part reverse.

Closed position. Travel forward stepping side to side on each beat (side touch, side touch). Turning counterclockwise, step side touch near instep, step side touch near instep, step side touch near instep, step side touch near instep.

Transition one-step to two-step or vice versa. The change of pattern is made when the feet are together.

Cajun Jitterbug

CAJUN JITTERBUG IS frequently danced to two-step music. The steps are smooth with many variations.

METER: 2/4. Directions are for man; women's part reverse.

Two hands joined. The basic step appears to be a "slight limp" with weight on right foot. Step left and lightly drag the right to the left, accent the second and fourth beats as the body drops (knees bend) ever so slightly. Step is smooth, (not a jerk or bounce). Step-close, step-close, (one and two and). The lead may change to right close, right close or during the moves, step alternately left, right on each beat like Four Count Swing, coming back into step close, step close. The arms push-pull like a parallelogram; arms held chest-high push to right side, pull left arm back, shift right side to right side and pivot clockwise using side close, side close or buzz step. Reverse to left side by side without losing a beat. The arms are never straight, sometimes referred to as "noodle arms."

The man leads the moves. All the figures are smooth, one leading to the next as the dancers cover a circular space. Refer to Swing, pages 42–55, for different figures. Additional figures resemble Bavarian Laendler.

Zydeco Two-Step

METER: 2/4. Steps based on eight counts. Directions are for man, woman's part reversed.
MUSIC: "Paper in My Shoe" by Boozoo Chavis; "Railroad Blues" by Lynn August; "Johnie Billie Goat" by Boozoo Chavis.

(Closed position)

STEPS	COUNTS	RHYTHM CUE
Moving in place, step left	1	Slow
Bend knee (slight bounce)	2	
Step right	3	Quick
Step left	4	Quick
Step right, bend knee (slight bounce)	5–6	Slow
Step left	7	Quick
Step right	8	Quick

STEP CUE: Step, drop, step, step; step, drop, step, step.

NOTE: Move in place. Travel forward in line of direction, stepping forward on counts 1 and 5. Turn clockwise or counterclockwise on counts 1 and 5.

STYLE: Keep steps small and controlled. Keep body accented downward, knees slightly bent, feet relatively flat on the floor with weight over the balls of the feet. Shoulders and arms are relatively still and parallel with the floor. The movements are gestures are smooth and subtle. The emphasis is more on the rhythm and footwork.

TEACHING SUGGESTIONS

Bounce in place 8 or 16 counts before starting step. Start with slow music. Repeat any variations 2 or 3 times to establish the pattern. Increase tempo. Steps are quick and light.

Variations

1. Closed position, 1 basic step. Repeat basic step, counts 1–6, then as man pushes left hand against woman's right hand (woman pushes right hand against man's left) man steps left foot behind his right, steps right in place and relaxes right hand, (counts 7–8). Woman steps right behind her left, steps left in place.
2. From closed position, move into Swing Out position and continue basic step. Keep joined hands and arms firm as basic step continues. Return to closed position on count 1.
3. Step on the toe, pivot or twist the heel in and out on counts 2 and 6. This is sometimes called "eat a beat."

Zydeco Two-Step (continued)

4. Brush (kick forward). Step left, brush right forward, step right, step left. Step right, brush left forward, step left, step right.
5. Closed position: step left turning clockwise, step right, left (slow, quick, quick). Open position: step right, brush left forward, step left, step right (quick, quick, quick, quick). Turn on the first step. Take two sets to make one complete turn.

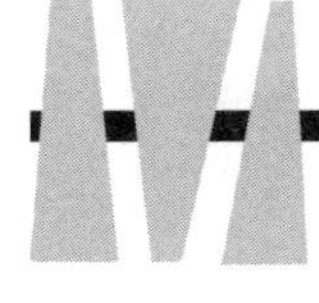

Tango

THE *TANGO* BEGAN as a raw, sensuous dance born on the Rio de la Plata in Buenos Aires amid the slums in a multiracial setting. In its earliest form, the name 'tan goo,' an onomatopetic rendition of the sounds of drums, strongly suggest its African origin. As with all dance forms, the Tango has passed through many evolutions. During its formative stages, it was a combination of *Candombe,* a syncopated African dance, the *Habanera,* and 18th century European dance, and the *Milango,* an indigenous Argentine dance.The Tango and its music was introduced to Paris and the Riviera by wealthy South Americans after World War I. It became the rage of Paris and it is from this setting and refinement that it spread throughout Europe and came to North America.

The 1990s have become the new age of the Tango. *Tangueros* are found in major cities around the world. Devotees attend workshops, organize weekly dances and practice to improve their skills while exchanging feelings and excitement about dancing the Argentine Tango. While maintaining its smooth sophisticated and suave style, the Tango's new charm lies in its improvised nature that relies on communication between partners rather than executing pre-learned step routines.

TANGO RHYTHM

The modern Tango is written in both 2/4 and 4/4 time. Here it will be presented 2/4 time.

2/4	S	S	Q	Q	S
	1	2	1	and	2

uneven rhythm

Basic tango rhythm

2/4	S	Q	Q
	1	2	and

uneven rhythm

Box step rhythm

2/4	Q	Q	S
	1	and	2

uneven rhythm

Twinkle rhythm

The Tango rhythm is a deliberate accented beat that is easily distinguished. Few dancers have trouble following the Tango rhythm. There is a calculated contrast between the slow promenade beats of the first measure and the staccato of the Tango break in the second measure.

TANGO STYLE

The Tango is characterized by a deliberate glide, not sliding the foot on the floor, but a long reach from the hip with a catlike smoothness and placement of the ball of the foot on the floor. The knees remain straight. The break, which is quick quick slow, is a sudden contrast ending in the subtle draw of the feet together. It is this combination of slow gliding beats and the sharp break that makes the Tango distinctive. Restraint is achieved by the use of continuous flow of movements and a controlled, stylized break presenting disciplined and sophisticated style, instead of a comic caricature. The dancer should strive to effect the idea of floating. Care should be taken to avoid the look of stiffness. Since the long reaching glide is used, the feet should pass each other close together. The draw in the Tango close is executed slowly, taking the full length of the slow beat to bring the feet together and then sweep quickly into the beginning of the basic rhythm again. The woman should synchronize the action of her drawing step with that of the man. The body and head are carried high and the woman's left hand, instead of being on the man's shoulder as in other dances, reaches around the man at his right shoulder–blade level. The fingers of the hand are straight and the arm is in a straight line from the elbow to the tip of the fingers.

Once in a while, deliberately move the shoulders forward in opposition to the feet. For example, stepping left, the right shoulder moves forward. The fan steps, most glamorous of all tango patterns, turn, whip, or swirl in almost exciting, subtle way. The fan style is described in detail with the variations used.

FUNDAMENTAL TANGO STEPS

Directions are for the man, facing the line of direction; the woman's part is reversed, except as noted.

■ BASIC TANGO STEP

(Closed position)

A combination of the promenade or walking step and the break.

STEPS	2/4 COUNTS	RHYTHM CUE
Step L forward	1	slow
Step R forward	2	slow
Step L in place	1	quick
Step R sideward abruptly	*and*	quick
Draw L to R, weight remains on R	2	slow

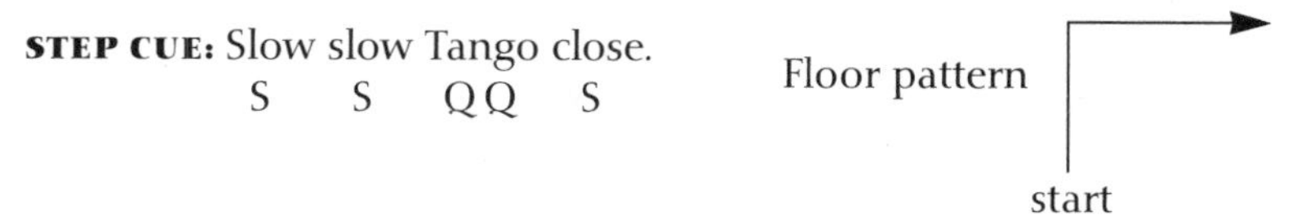

STYLE: The slow beats are long, smooth, gliding steps. The feet pass each other closely. The break quick quick slow is in place or slightly forward.

LEAD: Man must draw to the right with right hand and elbow to guide the woman in the break step.

NOTE: This step repeats each time from the man's left foot, because there is no change of weight on the draw. This pattern will tend to carry the couple outward toward the wall. It immediately becomes necessary to know how to vary the step in order to counteract this action. Open position, right parallel position, or quarter–turn all may be used for this purpose.

Fundamental Tango Steps (continued)

Tango Step Variations

Open Position Basic Tango	Half-Turn Clockwise	Right Parallel Basic Tango
The Box Step	Quarter-Turn	The Corté
Cross Step and Quarter-Turn	Open Fan	Half-Turn Counterclockwise

OPEN POSITION BASIC TANGO

(Closed position)

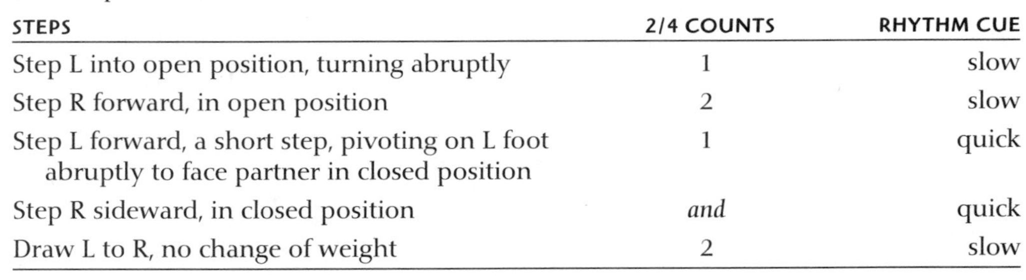

STEPS	2/4 COUNTS	RHYTHM CUE
Step L into open position, turning abruptly	1	slow
Step R forward, in open position	2	slow
Step L forward, a short step, pivoting on L foot abruptly to face partner in closed position	1	quick
Step R sideward, in closed position	*and*	quick
Draw L to R, no change of weight	2	slow

STEP CUE: Open step close side draw.

STYLE: The abrupt turning to open position on the first slow step and the turn back to closed position are sharp and only a firmness in the body can accomplish this.

LEAD: Refer to leads 7 and 8, p. 10. The lead is sudden and on the first slow beat.

RIGHT PARALLEL BASIC TANGO

(Closed position)

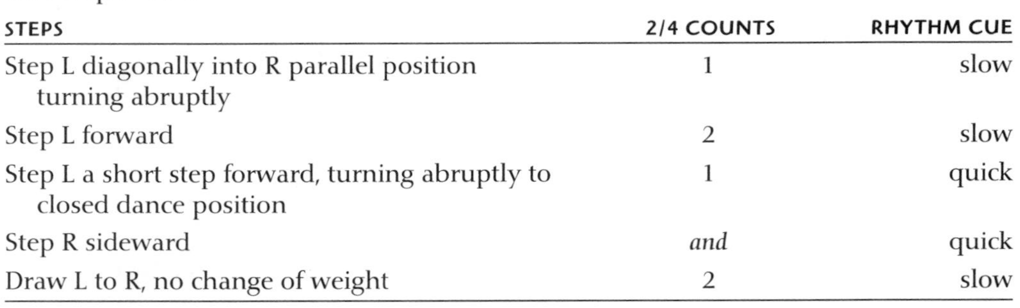

STEPS	2/4 COUNTS	RHYTHM CUE
Step L diagonally into R parallel position turning abruptly	1	slow
Step L forward	2	slow
Step L a short step forward, turning abruptly to closed dance position	1	quick
Step R sideward	*and*	quick
Draw L to R, no change of weight	2	slow

STEP CUE: Parallel step close side draw.

STYLE: Right parallel travels diagonally forward; woman's foot reaches parallel to man's left foot. The second slow is an exaggerated reaching step forward.

LEAD: To lead into right parallel position (left reverse open position) the man should not use pressure of his right hand, but rather should raise his right arm rotating the woman counterclockwise one-eighth of a turn while he rotates counterclockwise one-eighth of a turn. This places the man and woman off to the side of each other facing opposite directions. The woman is to the right of the man, but slightly in front of him. The man should avoid turning too far so as to be side by side as this results in poor style and awkward and uncomfortable motion. The man's left hand may assist the lead by pulling toward his left shoulder.

QUARTER-TURN

(Closed position)

STEPS	2/4 COUNTS	RHYTHM CUE
Step L forward	1	slow
Step R forward	2	slow
Step L, turning one-quarter counterclockwise	1	quick
Step R sideward	*and*	quick
Draw L to R, no change of weight	2	slow

■ CROSS STEP AND QUARTER-TURN

(Closed position)

STEPS	2/4 COUNTS	RHYTHM CUE
Step L sideward	1	slow
Step R across in front of L, take weight R	2	slow
Step L sideward, turn toe out, turn one-quarter counterclockwise	1	quick
Step R sideward	*and*	quick
Draw L to R, no change of weight	2	slow

STEP CUE: Side cross turn side close.

STYLE: All of this pattern is taken in closed position. The turn actually begins by a pivot on the crossing foot at the end of the second slow beat.

LEAD: Refer to Lead 12, p. 10.

■ HALF-TURN COUNTERCLOCKWISE

(Closed position)

STEPS	2/4 COUNTS	RHYTHM CUE
Step L into open position, turning abruptly	1	slow
Step R forward, a short step, pivoting one-quarter counterclockwise on the R foot; bring up R arm and turn the woman around the man a three-quarter turn to closed position	2	slow
Step L bringing L foot next to R foot	1	quick
Step R sideward	*and*	quick
Draw L to R, no weight change	2	slow

STEP CUE: Step pivot break side draw.

STYLE: The woman pivots counterclockwise on her left foot (second slow beat) around the man a three-quarter turn into closed position. The woman's step on this beat was a longer step than the man's, giving her freedom to pivot. She must bring her first quick step with R foot alongside of left foot.

LEAD: Man must bring up his right arm and elbow firmly, almost lifting her so that she can pivot easily on her left foot on the second slow beat.

■ HALF-TURN CLOCKWISE

(Closed position)

STEPS	2/4 COUNTS	RHYTHM CUE
Step L into open position, turning abruptly	1	slow
Step R forward, a long step, pivoting one-half clockwise on the R foot around the woman into closed position	2	slow
Step L sideward, a short step apart from where R foot is at the end of the pivot	1	quick
Step R sideward	*and*	quick
Draw L to R, no weight change	2	slow

Fundamental Tango Steps (continued)

STEP CUE: Step pivot break side draw.

STYLE: The man smoothly pivots on his right foot clockwise about halfway around the woman. The woman turns clockwise in place on her left foot. This step is very easy for the woman.

LEAD: Refer to lead indications 7 and 8, p. 10, for open and closed position. The main lead is increased resistance in hand, arm, and body as the man pivots halfway around the woman.

▪ DOUBLE CROSS

(In twinkle rhythm closed dance position)

STEPS	2/4 COUNTS	RHYTHM CUE
Step L sideways	1	slow
Step R across in front of L	2	slow
Point L sideways, take weight slightly	1	quick
Pivot hips to R with a slight push off with L, take weight R	*and*	quick
Swing L across in front of R, take weight L	2	slow
Point R to side	1	quick
Pivot hips to L with slight push off with R, take weight L	*and*	quick
Swing R across in front of L, take weight R	2	slow

STEP CUE: Side cross pivot and cross pivot and cross.
S S Q Q S Q Q S

STYLE: Stay in closed position throughout. Woman crosses in front, also.

LEAD: Firm body and arm control are needed to hold closed position.

NOTE: Finish with break side draw quick quick slow. This could also be done with the woman crossing behind.

▪ THE BOX STEP

The rhythm of the Tango box step is like that described in the Foxtrot–slow quick quick–forward side close, back side close.The Tango gliding action will be used on the first slow beat. The box step variations for Foxtrot may also be used here, including the box turn and the grapevine step. Refer to pp. 29, 30 and 32.

▪ THE CORTÉ

The corté is a dip, most often taken backward on the man's left or right foot. It is a type of break step used to finish off almost any Tango variation and is used as an ending to the dance. The skilled dancer will learn to use the corté in relationship to the music of the tango so that the feeling of the corté will correspond to the climax or the phrase of the musical accompaniment.

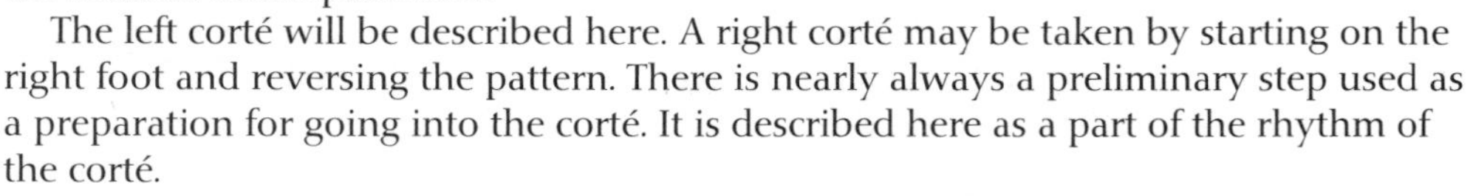

The left corté will be described here. A right corté may be taken by starting on the right foot and reversing the pattern. There is nearly always a preliminary step used as a preparation for going into the corté. It is described here as a part of the rhythm of the corté.

▪ PREPARATION STEP

STEPS	2/4 COUNTS	RHYTHM CUE
Step forward L, a short step	1	quick
Shift weight back onto R	*and*	quick

Corté

STEPS	2/4 COUNTS	RHYTHM CUE
Step L backward, take weight, and bend L knee slightly	2	slow
Recover forward, take weight R	1	slow
Step L in place beside R	2	quick
Step R in place beside L	*and*	quick

STEP CUE: Rock and dip recover quick quick.
Q Q S S Q Q

STYLE: As the *man* steps backward into the corté, the weight is all taken on the standing foot with a bent knee. The man should turn his bent knee slightly outward so that the woman's knee will not bump his as they go into the dip. His left shoulder and arm move forward (the left leg and left shoulder are in opposition). His back should remain straight. He should avoid leaning either backward or forward. His right foot should be extended (arched) so that the toe is only touching the floor.

The *woman* should step forward on the right, arch her back, and place all of her weight over the forward right foot. The right knee is bent. The left leg is extended behind and should be a straight line from hip to toe. A bent line makes the whole figure sag. The left arch of the foot should be extended so that the toe is pointed and remains in contact with the floor. If the woman steps forward too far or does not bend the forward knee, she will be forced to bend at the waist, which destroys the form of the figure. She may look back over her left shoulder. The execution of the dip should be as smooth as any slow backward step.The man should avoid leaping or falling back into the dip.

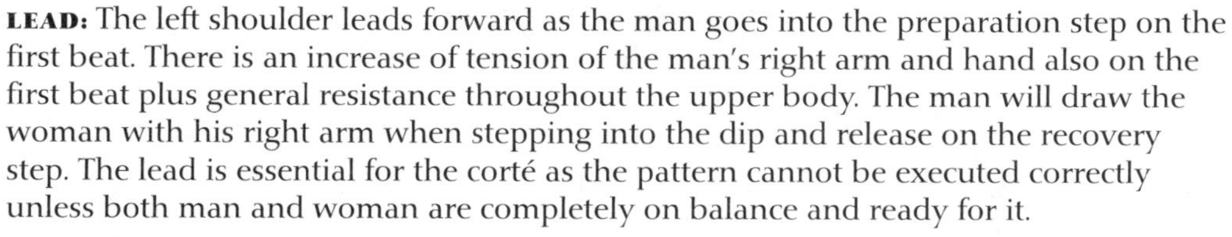

LEAD: The left shoulder leads forward as the man goes into the preparation step on the first beat. There is an increase of tension of the man's right arm and hand also on the first beat plus general resistance throughout the upper body. The man will draw the woman with his right arm when stepping into the dip and release on the recovery step. The lead is essential for the corté as the pattern cannot be executed correctly unless both man and woman are completely on balance and ready for it.

NOTE: The recovery step is followed by two quick steps left right, which finish count 2 and complete the measure of music. These may be omitted when they follow a variation that takes up those extra counts. Learn the footwork first, then work on the style.

▪ FAN STEP

The fan is a term used to describe a manner of executing a leg motion, in which the free leg swings in a whiplike movement around a small pivoting base. This should not be a large sweeping movement in a wide arc but rather a small subtle action initiated in the hip and executed with the legs close together. The balance is carefully poised over the pivoting foot at all times. When the man and woman take the fan motion, the action is taken parallel to partner; that is, the right leg, which is free, swings forward. When it reaches its full extension, just barely off the floor, the right hip turns the leg over, knee down, while pivoting on the standing foot to face the opposite direction. The right leg then swings through forward and the weight is taken on the right foot. This action usually is done in slow rhythm. Accompanying the hip action there is also a lift and turn on the ball of the standing foot. This lift permits the free leg to swing through gracefully extended and close in a beautiful floating style.

Fundamental Tango Steps (continued)

■ OPEN FAN

(Open position)

STEPS	2/4 COUNTS	RHYTHM CUE
Step L forward	1	slow
Step R forward	2	slow
Step L in place, releasing R arm around woman, and turn halfway around to the right to a side-by-side position with woman on man's L	1	quick
Step R sideward, a short step	*and*	quick
Draw L to R, no weight change (the man's L hand is holding the woman's R)	2	slow
Step forward L	1	quick
Swing the R leg forward, pivoting on L foot while fanning the R, coming halfway around to open position	*and*	quick
Step forward R in open position	2	slow
Step L forward, pivoting toward the woman into closed position	1	quick
Step R sideward	*and*	quick
Draw L to R, no weight change	2	slow

STEP CUE: Slow slow open side draw/fan through break side draw

STYLE: When the man releases his arm around her, the woman turns halfway around to the left. On the fan, the woman steps right, swings left leg forward, hip turns over, knee faces down. Foot is kept close to the floor and sweeps through pivoting clockwise to open position, and weight is transferred forward onto left foot. She then goes into break step with partner.

LEAD: The man drops his right arm and pulls away from the woman to side-by-side position. Then, with his left hand, he pulls in as he fans through to open position and from there lifts his right arm into closed position for Tango close.

NOTE: This is an easy beginner step in fan style and gives them the thrill of the Tango.

■ GRAPEVINE FAN

(Starting in open position)

STEPS	2/4 COUNTS	RHYTHM CUE
Step L forward	1	slow
Rock forward and back R, L	*2 and*	quick quick
Step R backward rising on R toe and lifting L leg just off the floor	1	slow
Step L backward, turning toward partner	2	quick
Step R sideward, turning to face reverse open position	*and*	quick
Step L forward in reverse open position	1	quick
Fan R leg forward and through to open position	*and*	quick
Step R forward, in open position	2	slow
Step L forward, a short step, turning to closed position	1	quick
Step R sideward	*and*	quick
Draw L to R, no weight change	2	slow

STEP CUE: Step rock and back grapevine step fan through break side close.
S Q Q S Q Q Q Q S Q Q S

STYLE: The couple should not get too far apart or lean forward to maneuver this grapevine pattern. They should stand upright and keep carefully balanced over standing foot. The fanning leg swings in line with the travelling and facing action, not in a side arc. The legs are kept close together.

LEAD: This is a pattern man and woman must know together but the man cues the woman by use of both hands and use of his body in turning from one position to another.

NOTE: This is a beautiful pattern when used following the forward and open rock.

▪ PARALLEL FAN

(Fan style in parallel position; starting in closed dance position)

STEPS	2/4 COUNTS	RHYTHM CUE
Man's Part: Starts and ends in closed position. Starting L, take one basic Tango step, slow slow quick quick slow.		
Step L forward	1	slow
Step R sideward turning to open position	2	quick
Step L to R, taking weight L	*and*	quick
Step R forward, turning woman to R parallel position	1	slow
Rock backward onto L, turning woman to open position	2	slow
Rock forward onto R, turning woman to R parallel position	1	slow
Rock back onto L, turning woman to open position	2	slow
Step R forward in open position	1	slow
Take Tango–close step, turning to closed position	2 *and* 1	quick quick slow
Woman's Part: Starting right, take one basic tango step, slow slow quick quick slow.		
Step R backward	1	slow
Step L sideward, turning to open position	2	quick
Step R to L, taking weight on R	*and*	quick
Step L forward (fan), pivoting to R parallel position	1	slow
Step R forward (fan), pivoting to open position	2	slow
Step L forward (fan), pivoting to R parallel position	1	slow
Step R forward (fan), pivoting to open position	2	slow
Step L forward (fan), pivoting to R parallel position	1	slow
Step R forward (fan), pivoting to open position	2	slow
Step L forward, turning to closed position	1	slow
Take Tango close	2 *and* 1	quick quick slow

STEP CUE: With slow and quick rhythm except for the fan: rock rock rock rock/forward break side draw.

STYLE: The steps are small in the fan part of the step so that the woman may turn without reaching for the step. The man in the fan part of the step rocks forward, back, forward, back in place, as he turns the woman. She takes her fan, pivoting alternately on the left, right, left, right, swinging the free leg forward a short distance until the toe just clears the floor and then turning the hip with her pivot to the new direction and reaching through for the next step. The woman should rise slightly on her toe as she pivots. This smooths out the turn and makes one of the most beautiful movements in Tango.

Fundamental Tango Steps (continued)

LEAD: Man's first lead will be to lower right arm into open position. He then guides her forward with his right hand, moving her alternately from right parallel position to open position until the end when he raises his right arm and turns her to closed position.

NOTE: A corté may be added to this figure instead of the Tango close by stepping through to open position on the R (count 1), turning the woman quickly to closed position, rocking forward and back (counts 2 *and*); corté (count 1), recover onto the L foot (count 2) and finish with Tango close (counts 1 and 2).

TANGO COMBOS

The Tango routines are combinations for practice, listed from simple to complex. (Closed position, unless otherwise indicated.)

1. *Basic*
   2 basic steps
   1 basic step (open position)
2. *Basic, Cross Step*
   2 basic steps
   4 cross steps and quarter-turn
3. *Box, Basic, Cross Step*
   2 box steps
   1 basic step
   1 cross step and quarter-turn
4. *Basic, Cross, Corté*
   2 basics
   1 cross step, quarter-turn
   1 corté
5. *Advanced Combo*
   2 box steps
   1 basic
   1 cross step
   open fan
6. *Advanced Combo*
   2 basics
   open fan
   half-turn clockwise
   corté
   1 basic

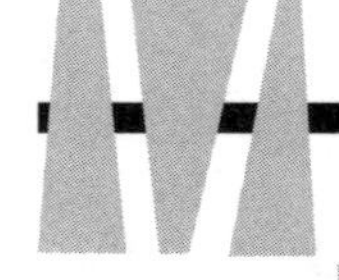

Waltz

ALTHOUGH A MAJORITY of the middle European countries lay some claim to the origin of the *Waltz*, the world looked to Germany and Austria, where the great Waltz was made traditional by the beautiful music of Johann Strauss and his sons. It has a pulsating, swinging rhythm, which has been enjoyed by dancers everywhere, even by those who dance it only in its simplest pattern, the Waltz Turn. Its immediate popularity and its temporary obscurity are not unlike other fine inheritances of the past, which come and go with the ebb and flow of popular accord. Early use of the Waltz in America was at the elegant social balls and cotillions. Its outstanding contribution to present-day dancing is the Waltz position. Even in its early stages, it was quite some time before this position was socially acceptable. Now the closed position is universally the basic position for Ballroom Dancing.

The Waltz music is played in three different tempos–slow, medium, and fast. The slow or medium Waltz is preferred by most people. However, the fast Waltz is a favorite of those who know the Viennese style. The slower American style is danced for the most part on a box pattern, but the use of other variations has added a new interest.

WALTZ RHYTHM

The Waltz is played in 3/4 time. It is three beats per measure of music, with an accent on the first beat. The three beats of Waltz time are very even, each beat receiving the same amount of time. The three movements of the Waltz step pattern blend perfectly with the musical tempo or beat of each measure. The tempo may be slow, medium, or fast.

3/4 | slow slow slow

1 2 3

even rhythm

Slow box rhythm

Canter rhythm in Waltz time is a means of holding the first and second beats together so the resultant pattern is an uneven rhythm, or slow quick slow quick. It is counted 1, 3, 1, 3.

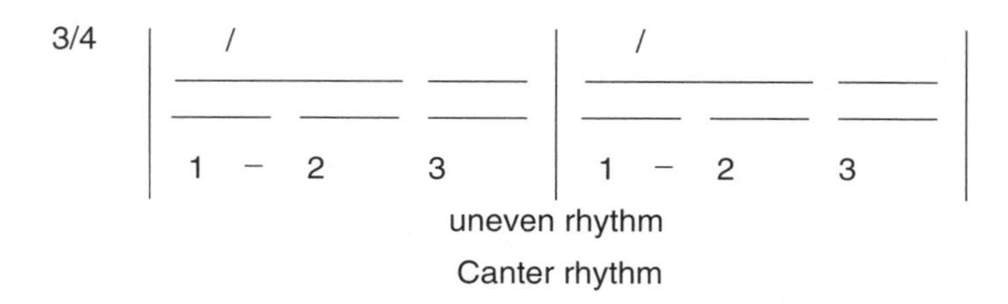

uneven rhythm

Canter rhythm

The Viennese Waltz is an even three-beat rhythm, played very fast. It is a turning pattern. There is only one step on the first beat of the measure and a pivot of the body on that foot for the two remaining counts of the measure.

3/4 | step pivot

1 2 3

even rhythm

Viennese rhythm

WALTZ STYLE

The Waltz is a smooth dance with a gliding quality that weaves an **even pattern** of swinging and turning movement. The first accented beat of the music is also accented in the motion. The first step of the Waltz pattern is the reaching step forward, backward, sideward, or turning. Because it is the first beat that gives the dance its new impetus, its new direction, or a change of step, there evolves a pulsating feeling, which can be seen rather markedly and is the chief characteristic of the beauty of the Waltz. This should not be interpreted as a rocking or bobbing motion of the body. On count 1, the man steps *flat* on the sole of the foot; on counts 2–3, the body rises stepping on the ball of the foot. The rising action is sometimes described as a *lift*. The "fall and rise" action of the body is seen in every step. The footwork is most effective when the foot taking the second beat glides past the standing foot as it moves into the sideward step. The feet should never be heard to scrape the floor, but should seem to float in a silent pattern. In closed position, it is important for the woman to be directly in front of the man, their shoulders parallel.

Waltz (continued)

FUNDAMENTAL WALTZ STEPS

Directions are for the man, facing line of direction; woman's part is reversed, except as noted.

■ BOX STEP

(Closed position)

STEPS	3/4 COUNTS	STYLE CUE
Step L forward	1	flat
Step R sideward, passing close to the L foot	2	lift
Close L to R, take weight L	3	lift
Step R backward	1	flat
Step L sideward, passing close to the R foot	2	lift
Close R to L, take weight R	3	lift

STEP CUE: Forward side close/back side close.

STYLE: The forward step is **on the heel.** Follow through on the second beat, moving the free foot closely past the standing foot, but do not lose a beat by stopping. Body rises on counts 2, 3 as stepping on ball of foot. The floor pattern is a long narrow rectangle rather than a square box.

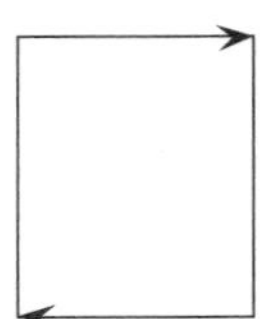

Floor pattern

LEAD: To lead a box step the man should use a forward body action followed by right-hand pressure and right elbow pull to the right to take the woman into the forward sequence of the box. Forward pressure of the right hand followed by pressure to the left side takes the woman into the back sequence of the box.

NOTE: The man must understand the concept of the forward side close as being the forward sequence of the box and the backward side close as being the back sequence of the box. This terminology will be used in future patterns.

■ BOX TURN

(Left)–(Closed position)

STEPS	3/4 COUNTS	STYLE CUE
Step L forward, toe out, turning one-quarter L	1	flat
Step R sideward, gliding past the L foot	2	lift
Close L to R, taking weight L	3	lift
Step R backward, toe in, turning one-quarter L	1	flat
Step L sideward, gliding past the R foot	2	lift
Close R to L, taking weight R	3	lift
Step L forward, toe out, turning one-quarter L	1	flat
Step R sideward, gliding past the L foot	2	lift
Close L to R, taking weight on L	3	lift
Step R backward, toe in, turning one-quarter L	1	flat
Step L sideward, gliding past the R foot	2	lift
Close R to L, taking weight R	3	lift

STEP CUE: Turn side close, turn side close.

WOMAN: The woman is taking the reverse pattern, except that, when the woman steps forward with the left foot, instead of toeing out as described for the man, she steps forward between the man's feet, her left foot next to the instep of the man's left foot. This style greatly facilitates the turn.

MAN: A common error is that the man tries to step around his partner. The woman must be directly in front of her partner.

STYLE: Accent the first step by reaching with a longer step. However, man must be careful not to overreach his partner. There is no unnecessary knee bending or bobbing up and down.

LEAD: To lead a box turn with slight pressure of the right hand, the man should use the right arm and shoulder to guide or bank the woman into the turn. The shoulders press forward during the forward step and draw backward during the backward step.

NOTE: For the right turn, start with the right foot. Follow the same pattern with opposite footwork.

■ *Teaching Strategy for Changing Leads—Turn Right, Turn Left*

It is important to learn to turn counterclockwise and clockwise. The foot must be free to *lead* in the direction of the turn: left lead for left turn; right lead for right turn. There are several ways to change the lead. With the left, step balance or a hesitation step, then start the box with the right foot (right side close, left side close). Another is to take two Waltz steps forward, take the third Waltz step backward; right foot is now free to turn right. To return to the left lead, either step (R) balance or take two Waltz steps forward and the third one backward; then the left foot leads again. Once the student can turn left and right, the teacher should present a definite routine that drills this change. When students learn this concept for the Waltz, they will be able to transfer the principle to other rhythms.

■ *Waltz Step Variations*

Hesitation Step	Weaving Step	Streamline Step
Cross Step	Twinkle Step	Viennese Waltz

■ HESITATION STEP

(Closed position)

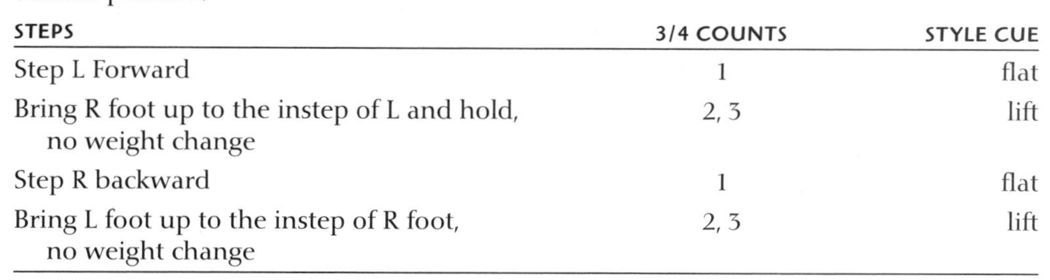

STEPS	3/4 COUNTS	STYLE CUE
Step L Forward	1	flat
Bring R foot up to the instep of L and hold, no weight change	2, 3	lift
Step R backward	1	flat
Bring L foot up to the instep of R foot, no weight change	2, 3	lift

STEP CUE: Step close hold.

STYLE: Smooth.

LEAD: To lead a hesitation step the man dips his shoulder in the direction of the turn, and his upper torso turns before his leg and foot turn.

NOTE: As in the Foxtrot, a beautiful combination is to dance two hesitation steps, then the first half of the box turn, two hesitation steps and then the second half of the turn. The hesitation step repeated may also be done turning either counterclockwise or clockwise and may be useful in maneuvering for the next step.

Fundamental Waltz Steps (continued)

▪ CROSS STEP

(Closed position)

STEPS	3/4 COUNTS	STYLE CUE
Step L forward	1	flat
Step R sideward, turning to open position	2	lift
Close L to R, taking weight L	3	lift
Step R forward, in open position	1	flat
Step L forward, turning on L foot to face partner in closed position	2	lift
Close R to L, taking weight R	3	lift

STEP CUE: Forward side close, cross side close.

STYLE: The position is opened to semiopen position, just enough to step forward on the inside foot, which feels like a crossing step. It should be accented by a long, smooth, reaching step on the heel, not a dipping or bobbing action.

LEAD: To lead into an open position or conversation position, the man should use pressure with the heel of the right hand to turn the woman into open position. The right elbow lowers to the side. The man must simultaneously turn his own body, not just the woman so that they end facing the same direction. The left arm relaxes slightly and the left hand sometimes gives the lead for steps in the open position.

LEAD: To lead from open to closed position the man should use pressure of the right hand and raise the right arm up to standard position to move the woman into closed position. The woman should not have to be pushed but should swing easily into closed position as she feels the arm lifting. She should move completely around to face the man squarely.

NOTE: When man is facing out in closed position, he can go into this step and the cross pattern will travel in line of direction.

▪ WEAVING STEP

Same as cross step but crossing from side to side. (Closed position)

STEPS	3/4 COUNTS	STYLE CUE
Step L forward	1	flat
Step R sideward, turning to open position	2	lift
Close L to R, taking weight L	3	lift
Step R forward in open position	1	flat
Step L forward, turning to side-by-side position facing the reverse line of direction	2	lift
Close R to L, taking weight R	3	lift
Step L forward, in side-by-side position	1	flat
Step R forward, turning to open position	2	lift
Close L to R, taking weight L	3	lift
Step R forward in open position	1	flat
Step L forward, turning to closed position	2	lift
Close R to L, taking weight R	3	lift

STEP CUE: Forward side open/cross side reverse/cross side revere/cross side close.

STYLE: Reach into crossing step on the heel. It is a long reaching step on the accented beat.

LEAD: Turn woman to semiopen position for first cross step and then drop right arm and lead through with the left hand to side-by-side position, facing the reverse line of direction. Next time, as they reverse direction, the man puts his arm around her in open position and follows standard procedure for returning to closed position.

NOTE: The weave pattern may be repeated back and forth, crossing as many times as desired, but should go back to closed position as described above.

▪ TWINKLE STEP

(Closed position)

It is led from the back sequence of the box step.

STEPS	3/4 COUNTS	STYLE CUE
Step L forward	1	flat
Step R sideward turning into R parallel position	2	lift
Close L to R, taking eight L	3	lift
Step R, diagonally forward in R parallel position	1	flat
Step L sideward, turning from R parallel to L parallel position	2	lift
Close R to L, taking weight R	3	lift
Step L diagonally forward in L parallel position	1	flat
Step R sideward, turning from L parallel position to R parallel position	2	lift
Close L to R, taking weight on L	3	lift
Step R diagonally forward in R parallel position	1	flat
Step L sideward turning to closed position	2	lift
Close R to L, taking weight on R	3	lift

Floor pattern

start

STEP CUE: Step turn close.

STEP CUE: The second beat has a short step and a smooth roll from one position to another. The woman reaches parallel to the man's step, except that she is stepping diagonally backward, which takes a lot of practice for the woman to do it well.

LEAD: To lead into right parallel position (left reverse open position) the man should not use pressure of his right hand, but rather should raise his right arm rotating the woman counterclockwise one-eighth of a turn while he rotates counterclockwise one-eighth of a turn. This places the man and woman off to the side of each other facing opposite directions. The woman is to the right of the man but slightly in front of him. The man should avoid turning too far so as to be side by side as this results in poor style and awkward and uncomfortable motion. The man's left hand may assist the lead by pulling toward his left shoulder.

LEAD: To lead from right parallel position to left parallel position (right reverse open position), the man should pull with his right hand lowering the right arm and push slightly with his left hand causing a rotation clockwise about a quarter of a turn until the woman is to the left of him but slightly in front of him. They are not side by side.

NOTE: Progress is in a zigzag pattern down the floor in the line of direction and may repeat over and over as desired.

▪ *Suggestions for Variations*

Any student or teacher who has followed these directions this far should be prepared to make use of the advance twinkle, corté, and pivot turn described under the Foxtrot by transposing a slow, quick, quick in 4/4 time into slow, slow, slow in 3/4 time. Refer to corte p. 28, Twinkle p. 31, Pivot Turn pp. 32, 33.

Fundamental Waltz Steps (continued)

■ STREAMLINE STEP

(Closed position)

An advanced step seen in the International Style and competition. Dancers travel in the line of direction and need a lot of space to move. Step on every beat, each step forward. The feet are never together, always moving forward! Step flat on the first beat; body rises on counts 2–3. The floor pattern, although forward, zigs and zags. In addition to moving forward, the dancers may rock or grapevine.

ROCK: Forward, backward, forward; backward, forward, backward.

GRAPEVINE: Semiopen position, travel in line of direction.

■ VIENNESE WALTZ

The **rhythm** is three even, quick beats now instead of slow. The Viennese Waltz music is fast and it is hard to keep one's balance on the pivot step when it is slowed down, so that students get discouraged learning the step. An experiment of a half-Viennese has proved successful in getting students to learn the pivot step by doing it first on the right foot and then taking a regular Waltz step on the left sequence.

3/4	step	side	cross	step	pivot	
	1	2	3	1	2	3
	quick	quick	quick	right	pivot	

Half-Viennese step

Half-Viennese Step:

1. Both man and woman need to practice this pattern alone, traveling down line of direction.

STEPS	3/4 COUNTS	RHYTHM CUE
Step L forward, turning one-quarter counterclockwise	1	quick
Step R sideward, turning one-quarter counterclockwise	2	quick
Slide the L foot, heel first, in across R to the R of the R foot. Transfer weight to L foot. Both toes are facing the reverse line of direction, feet are crossed	3	quick
Step R backward and pivot one-half counterclockwise on the R foot	1	quick
Bring the L foot up to the instep of the R foot and with the L toe help balance on the R foot	2, 3	quick quick
2. Closed position, the man facing the line of direction.		
Starting L, the man takes the step side cross while the woman, starting R, takes the back pivot	1, 2, 3	all quick
Starting R, the man takes the back pivot while the woman, starting L, takes step side across	1, 2, 3	all quick

STYLE: The couple remains in closed position throughout. The steps are small as the woman is turning on a small pivot base while the man takes step side cross. Since the man turns one-quarter on his forward step, his second step is in line of direction, a small step and cross on third beat. Then he steps back a short step and pivots while woman takes the step side cross. The dancers always progress in the line of direction. Use two Waltz steps for one complete turn. The body resistance is firm for both man and woman. They must lean away, pressing outward but keeping the center of gravity over the pivoting feet. The shoulders tilt slightly in on direction and then the other; tilt left as the left foot leads, right as the right foot leads. Do not resist the momentum of body weight, but rather give into the momentum.

LEAD: Firm body and arms in correct position. The momentum comes from the rapid transfer of the body forward in the line of direction every time on count 1.

CUE: 1, 2, 3, 1, 2, 3.

Viennese Step:

3. The true Viennese with a step pivot repeated over and over is in closed dance position. Man starting L forward, woman R backward.

STEPS	3/4 COUNTS	RHYTHM CUE
Step L forward, pivoting on the ball of the foot one-half counterclockwise; the right foot coming up to the instep of the L and with the R toe, helps to balance on the L foot	1, 2, 3	all quick
Step R backward, pivoting on the ball of the foot one-half counterclockwise; the L foot coming to the instep of the R helps to balance on the R foot	1, 2, 3	all quick

STEP CUE: Step pivot, step pivot.

STYLE: There is a lift of the body going into the pivot, which lifts the body weight, momentarily allowing the feet to pivot with less weight. Take care not to throw the weight off balance.

LEAD: Same as above.

VARIATIONS: The hesitation step as given under the box pattern is very helpful in giving a rest from the constant turning. Also, by using an uneven number of hesitation steps, the right foot is free and the whole Viennese turn may be changed to a clockwise turn starting with the right foot and applying the pattern with opposite footwork.

WALTZ COMBOS

These Waltz routine are combinations for practice, listed from simple to complex. (Closed position, unless otherwise indicated.)

1. *Balance and Box*
   2 balance steps
   (forward, backward)
   4 box steps
2. *Waltz Box*
   1 box step
   2 forward Waltz steps
   1 box turn
3. *Cross Box and Turn*
   2 cross steps
   1 box turn
4. *Hesitation and Box Turn*
   2 hesitation steps
   (forward, backward)
   1 box turn
5. *Cross Step and Weaving*
   2 cross steps
   1 weaving step
6. *Advanced Combo*
   1 box turn
   4 twinkle steps
   2 hesitation steps
   2 pursuit Waltz steps
   1 corté
   1 forward Waltz step
7. *Advanced Combo*
   6 streamline steps (18 beats)
   2 twinkle steps
   4 streamline steps
   2 hesitation steps

3 Country Western Dance

Country Western

COUNTRY WESTERN DANCE has been around for a long time; it is definitely a grass-roots dance. As country western music has increased in popularity so has Country Western Dance. Country western music, a twangy honky-tonk sound as played by Bob Wills and his Texas Playboys in the late 1930s, was just the beginning. The music is influenced by spirituals, Dixieland jazz, and the big band sound. The fiddle, steel guitar, and deep bass give country western music its character. The fiddle was part of the band. Wherever country western music is played, people dance. The dances are based on old Folk Dances, Square Dances, and Social Dances, topped off with a new look, called Country Western. *Swing, One-Step, Two-Step, Schottische, Waltz,* and *Line Dances* are all part of the repertory.

COUNTRY WESTERN STYLE

The dance is very smooth, gliding and elegant. The upper body is quiet, with a straight back and very little hip movement; the knees are slightly bent, and are used as a spring to lower the center of gravity; the feet stay close to the floor. There is no pumping of the hands, no bounce, no waddle. In closed position, the dancers are apart. A relaxed, friendly, easygoing attitude is ever present.

The country western look starts with cowboy boots for both men and women. The men frequently wear Levis, and are proud of their large silver belt buckles. Many dance with their cowboy hats on. One writer commented that real cowboys now wear caps that say "Coors," "Mac," or "Bull Durham." Nonetheless, it is the Stetson type one sees on the dance floor. The women also enjoy wearing Levis or a western skirt, cowboy shirt or blouse, and scarves.

When the man has one or two hands free, he inserts his thumb into his belt, near the buckle, fingers pointing down casually. The woman may put her thumb in her belt too, or, if both hands are free as in a line dance, behind her back. She overlaps them, palms facing out, which is typical of Mexican-style dance.

COUNTRY WESTERN MUSIC

Country Line dances may be danced to any popular country tune. The exceptions, "Achy Breaky" and "Cotton-Eyed Joe," are danced to the tune by the same name. When a particular tune fits well to the step routine, a match is made. Then the routine takes the name of the tune, for example, "Elvira." Obviously the Waltz, Schottische, One-Step, Swing, and Two-Step need the correct meter.

DANCE-HALL ETIQUETTE

At country western dances, several types of dancing may take place simultaneously. The perimeter of the dance floor is for round dances; the slower ones dance in the inside lane. Fast and slow dancers move counterclockwise around the floor. The Swing Dancers and Line Dancers split the center area, with line dancers closer to the band.

The man takes the woman's hand, arm, or offers his arm to escort her onto or off the dance floor and to return her to her seat. The man always leads; the woman follows graciously.

In Western and Cajun dancing it is customary to leave the dance floor and return to your table or side of the room, even if you plan to dance the next dance with the same partner. The man still takes the woman's hand or arm and offers his arm to escort her onto and off the dance floor and to return to her seat. The man usually leads the way to and from the dance floor.

Country Swing

COUNTRY SWING RHYTHM

The music is the primary difference between *Country Swing, Disco Swing,* and *Swing.* The syncopated rhythm of rock and roll permeates the country western music for Swing.

Country Swing is danced to faster, 2/4 or 4/4 time, western music. There is 4-count, 6-count, and 8-count swing. The 4-count swing has a smooth, even rhythm, and is especially comfortable for learning all the figures. The 6-count swing (Double Lindy) also has an even rhythm. The 8-count swing (Triple Lindy) has uneven rhythm. For analysis and dance directions of Double and Triple Lindy refer to pp. 45–50 and pp. 50–52.

TERMINOLOGY

DOUBLE LINDY	*COUNTRY SWING*
Collegiate	Basic 6-Count Swing
Swing Out Break	Outside Turn
Continuous Underarm turns	Inside Turns
Brush Off	Brush Off
Tuck Spin	Free Spin
Wrap	Wrap, Basket, Cradle, Curl, Cuddle, Sweetheart
Double Brush Off	Double Brush Off, Double Brush
Dish Rag	Barrel Roll, Egg Beater
Overhead Swing	Slide
Triple Lindy Swivel Steps	Double Two-Step

TEACHING SUGGESTION: Teach the figures first. Then add the basic step pattern.

Texas Two-Step Swing

POSITION: Two hands joined.

Directions are for the man; the woman's part is reversed.

STEPS	4/4 COUNTS	STEP CUE
Step L in place	1	step
Touch R to L	2	touch
Step R in place	3	step
Touch L to R	4	touch
Step L backward, a little behind R heel	1	rock
Step R forward	2	step

FIGURES: Swing out position. The variations occur on the first 4 counts.

1. Woman turns clockwise under her R arm, in place.
2. Man turns clockwise under his L arm in place.
3. Man and woman exchange places as he turns her counterclockwise across to his position and steps around her to her position.
4. Two hands joined. Man raises L arm, woman steps R toward partner, turning counterclockwise under his arm, steps L as she is side by side on his R. Lower man's L, woman's R arms. Now in Cuddle position (Wrap). Rock, step. In this position, dancers may go forward, travel clockwise or counterclockwise in place dancing the Texas Two-Step. To unwrap, the man initiates a reverse roll, turning the woman clockwise back to starting position. Refer to page 49.

Cotton-Eyed Joe

DOROTHY SCARBOROUGH IDENTIFIES *Cotton-Eyed Joe* as an authentic slavery tunesong in her book *On the Trail of Negro Folksongs.* One that antebellum blacks played and sang was one that dealt with Cotton-Eyed Joe. Judging by the many verses—all in the same vein—he was a tantalizing, intriguing, and devilish character.

Hadn't been for Cotton-Eyed Joe
I'd 'a' been married twenty years ago
With an old gourd fiddle and a cornstalk bow
None could play like Cotton-Eyed Joe.

The fiddle tune, written in 2/4 meter, may be found in several references, one being Ira W. Ford's *Traditional Music of America.* Some references present the same tune in 4/4 meter. Today the bands give "Cotton-Eyed Joe" a Country Western flavor. The schot-tische usually follows "Cotton-Eyed Joe."

RECORDS: Belco 257; Kik-R, K-202

CASSETTES: DC 162105; MH 35, C 74.

MUSIC: Dave, Red River, "Cotton-Eyed Joe," Southern Music Co., San Antonio, TX.

POSITION: Varsouvienne

STEPS: Kick, Two-Step, push step.

DIRECTIONS FOR THE COUPLE DANCE

METER: 2/4. Directions are the same for man and woman.

■ MEASURES

I. Kicker

1 Beginning left, cross left foot and knee in front of right knee; kick left foot forward.
2 Back up, taking one Two-Step.
3–4 Beginning right, repeat action of measures 1–2.
5–8 Repeat action of measures 1–4.

II. Two-Step

9–16 Beginning left, take eight Two-Steps in line of direction.

Improvisation may take place in part II, such as turning, backing up, or walking around.

Cotton-Eyed Joe (continued)

DIRECTIONS FOR THE LINE DANCE

FORMATION: Lines of three, four, six, or as many as desired, arms around neighbor's waist, facing line of direction. Lines move like spokes in a wheel. Or lines of two in Varsouvienne or Promenade position.

STEPS: Kick, Two-Step.

METER: 2/4. Directions are same for man and lady.

The action is the same as for the Couple Dance above.

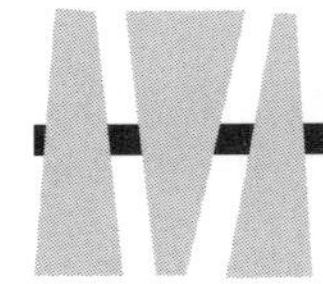

Ten-Step

TEN-STEP IS ALSO known as *Ten-Step Polka.* A similar dance, 8 beats, is the Jessie Polka. Country western dancers call the Jessie Polka the *Eight-Step Shuffle* or *Cowboy Polka.*

METER: 2/4 fast or 4/4 slow. Directions are presented in beats.

RECORD: Grenn 25371.

MUSIC: Fiddle music; suggested tunes: "Uncle Pen," "Cajun Moon," "New Cut Road," "On the Road Again," "East Bound and Down."

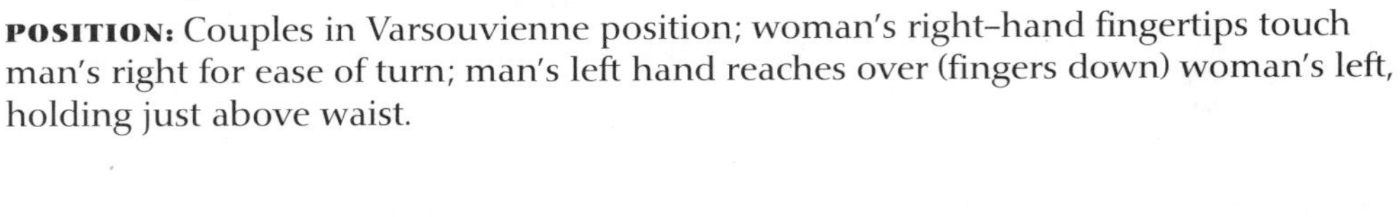

POSITION: Couples in Varsouvienne position; woman's right-hand fingertips touch man's right for ease of turn; man's left hand reaches over (fingers down) woman's left, holding just above waist.

DIRECTIONS FOR THE DANCE

■ *Beats*

Part I

1–2 Beginning left—right knee bent—touch left heel forward, left foot turned to a 45° angle, and return. Shift weight to left.

3 Touch right toe backward.

4 Brush (scuff) right heel as returning (no weight).

5	Touch right heel forward, right foot turned to a 45° angle.
6	Sweep right, heel leading, across in front of left.
7–8	Touch right heel forward, right foot turned to a 45° angle, and return, taking weight.
9	Touch left heel forward, left foot turned to a 45° angle.
10	Sweep left, heel leading, across in front of right.
	Part II
11–18	Beginning left, take four Two-Steps forward in line of direction (quick, quick, slow—four times).

STYLE: Review Line Dance style, p. 90. Knees are slightly bent, keep the dance smooth.

■ *Variations for Part II*

Part I is referred to as "think steps" because the leader decides what variation to do. During Part II partners may improvise with a wide variety of maneuvers. The number of Two-Steps may be increased by an even number.

1. Woman turns under man's left arm once or twice while moving forward.
2. Man lifts right hand over woman's head, woman taking four Two-Steps turns toward the man, and moves to his left side to face line of direction in promenade position. Repeat Part II; then man raises his right arm over his head like a lariat and woman taking four Two-Steps travels behind the man. She starts to turn counterclockwise 360° (third Two-Step); her right shoulder comes to his right shoulder; man lifts his left arm up and extends his right arm down at his side, shoulder to shoulder; she pivots to face forward in original position (fourth Two-Step).
3. *The Train.* Taking four Two-Steps, woman moves in front of man, two hands still joined and resting on her shoulders. Repeat Part II in this position. Woman Two-Steps back to place.
4. Take two Two-Steps forward; on the next two Two-Steps, the man raises his right arm over her head, and the woman travels in front of man to face him. Arms are crossed, extended and firm, with right hand on top. Repeat Part II. Pivoting counterclockwise, take four Two-Steps. Repeat Part II. Man lifts right arm over his head as she travels around behind him, turning 360° as in 2 to face original position.
5. *Wheel Around.* In Varsouvienne position, take four Two-Steps; the couple turns counterclockwise, the man dancing almost in place as the woman travels forward. Or turn clockwise, the woman dancing almost in place, as the man travels forward.

Texas Two-Step

THE *TEXAS TWO-STEP* IS also known as the *Texas Shuffle*. The dance is done in a smooth, flowing style. The rhythm—slow, slow, quick, quick—is referred to as *shuffle beat*. It is like the Foxtrot magic rhythm. The name is confusing because the real Two-Step, also done in Texas, is quick, quick, slow, or step-together-step.

TEXAS TWO-STEP RHYTHM

The music is written in 4/4 time. The step pattern takes a measure and a half of music. It is an uneven rhythm pattern—slow, slow, quick, quick.

4/4	S		S		Q	Q
	1	2	3	4	1	2

uneven rhythm

TEXAS TWO-STEP STYLE

The dance has smooth, controlled steps; there is no pumping of arms or bouncing. The closed dance position has several variations. The body has good posture alignment, with a straight back and knees slightly bent. Quite a bit of space should be left between partners in variations of the closed dance position. Man's left palm faces up and woman's right palm faces down, resting lightly in man's left; man's right arm may be straight, right hand folding over woman's left shoulder. The position of the woman's left arm varies. The woman may fold her left hand over his right elbow; her elbow is down, her arm is limp, which gives a "careless look." Her left arm may be extended to rest on top of man's right arm. Or she may hook her thumb into one of the man's belt loops on his right side. They face each other squarely, shoulders parallel.

The dancers glide around the floor in a counterclockwise direction and cover a lot of territory. Although there are many variations, most dancers relax and move forward, with an occasional turn, or the man dances backward, but always they move in the line of direction.

RECORDS: MH 35.

CASSETTE: MH C35.

MUSIC: Suggested tunes: "If It Was Easy" or "Everything a Waltz."

POSITION: Closed.

Directions are for the man; the woman's part is reversed.

STEPS	4/4 COUNTS	RHYTHM CUE
Step L forward	1–2	slow
Step R forward	3–4	slow
Step L forward	1	quick
Step R forward	2	quick

STYLE: The forward steps should be long, smooth, gliding steps, straight ahead. The woman moving backward, takes a long step, reaching from hip to toe. If the music is slow, for balance on the slow steps, dancers may step forward L, touch R to L (for balance), step forward R, touch L to R.

LEAD: A body and right-arm lead forward.

VARIATIONS: The variations usually start on the QQ.

1. Turn left to face the reverse line of direction, QQ.
2. Man travels backward in line of direction until ready to face the line of direction, then turn left on the QQ.
3. The man raises his left arm and the woman twirls clockwise under his arm, once or twice, on the QQ.
4. On the SS beats, step left to the side, step right to the side, travel forward QQ.
5. Open position, moving toward the center on the SS beats, step left, cross right in front of left. Closed position, travel left, right forward on the QQ.

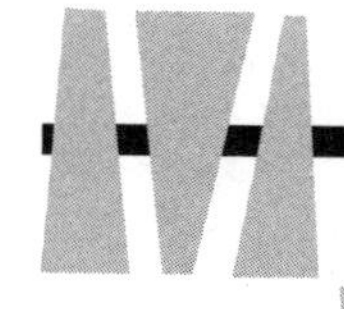

Traveling Cha Cha

METER: 4/4. Slow, Slow, Quick, Quick, Slow

Beats	1	2	3	&	4

MUSIC: "I Like It, I Love It" by Tim McGraw, "Big Heart" by The Gibson Miller Band, "I'm Not Strong Enough to Say No" by Blackhawk.

POSITION: Varsouvienne Position.

DIRECTIONS FOR THE DANCE

■ *Beats*

1–2	Beginning left, rock forward and backward right.
3 & 4	Cha Cha. Shuffle backward left, right, left.
5–6	Rock backward right, rock forward left.
7 & 8	Cha Cha. Shuffle forward right, left, right.
1–4	Repeat action of beats 1–4 above.

Traveling Cha Cha (continued)

5–8	Repeat action of beats 5–8 above. On beats 7 & 8 raise right hands over woman's head while she turns one-half left to face man.
1–4	Man rocks forward left, backward right, cha, cha, cha; woman rocks forward left, backward right and on beats 3 & 4 cha, cha, cha turning one-half right under right hands to Varsouvienne Position.
5–8	Man rocks backward right, forward left, cha, cha, cha; woman rocks backward right, forward left, and on beats 7 & 8 cha, cha, cha turning one-half left to face man.
1–4	Man rocks forward left, backward right, cha cha, cha; woman rocks backward left, forward right, cha, cha, cha turning one-half right on beats 3 & 4 to Varsouvienne Position.
5–8	Both rock backward right, forward left, cha, cha, cha.
1–4	Rock forward left, backward right turning one-half right, beats 1–2, cha, cha, cha, facing reverse line of direction.
5–8	Rock forward right, backward left turning one-half left, beats 5–6, cha, cha, cha, facing line of direction.
1–8	Repeat action of beats 1–8 above.
1–2	Walking forward, step left, right, woman making full turn right under right hands.
3 & 4	Cha, cha, cha forward, left, right, left.
5–6	Walking forward, step right, left, woman making full turn left under right hands.
7 & 8	Cha, cha, cha forward, right, left, right.
1–8	Repeat action of beats 1–8 above.
1–2	Step left, right, woman crossing in front of man to his left side.
3–4	Beginning left, cha, cha, cha in place, dropping right hands, woman backs under man's left arm. Rejoins right hands behind man.
5–6	Step right, left, woman crossing behind man to his right side.
7 & 8	Beginning right, cha, cha, cha in place, dropping left hands, woman moves forward under man's right arm. Rejoin left hands in front of man.
1–8	Repeat action of beats 1–8 above.

Sweetheart Schottische

METER: 4/4. Directions are presented in beats.

MUSIC: "Queen of Memphis" by Confederate Railroad or any country song with a steady 4/4 beat.

POSITION: Varsouvienne position.

DIRECTIONS FOR THE DANCE

Beats

Starting position: Feet together, weight on right.

1–2 Beginning left, step forward, scuff right foot.

3–4 Step right forward, scuff left foot.

5–8 Step backward, left, right, left, scuff right foot.

9–10 Step right side with right foot, scuff left foot.

1–4 Grapevine left. Step side left, behind right, side left, scuff right foot.

5–8 Man: grapevine right, scuff left foot, lifting left hand to turn woman one-half clockwise.

Woman: step right, left, right, scuff left foot, turning one-half clockwise in front of man. End facing reverse line of direction and slightly to the left of man.

1–4 Man: lifting both hands to turn woman full turn counterclockwise, grapevine left and scuff right foot.

Woman: making full turn counterclockwise in front of partner step left, right left, scuff right foot. Ending facing reverse line of direction and slightly to the right of man.

5–8 Drop left hands.

Man: walk forward right, left, right, scuff left foot turning woman clockwise under joined right hands.

Woman: turning clockwise once and a half under joined right hands, step right, left, right, scuff left foot. End facing line of direction on man's right in Varsouvienne position.

NOTE: The action does not divide evenly into 8 counts; therefore, the pattern will not follow 8 count phrases.

4 Line Dance

Line Dance

LINE DANCE AS A specific dance form has become widely popular. It flourishes with equal enthusiasm in schools, dance halls, clubs, trailer parks, and senior centers. Its chief attraction lies in the fact that since a partner is not required everyone can participate. Formations are equally unencumbered, ranging from dancers simply scattered about the floor all facing one direction to lines and circles.

Line dance, or non-partner dances, dates from the deep recesses of time. In addition to its longevity as a form, it proves to be an excellent teaching device. Dancers have a chance to learn and practice uninhibited by a partner. It allows students a clear view of the demonstration of steps and in turn affords the teacher an equally good view of student reaction and progress. As currently performed, some dances face a different direction or wall on each repetition and are referred to as "four wall line dances."

Many of the popular novelty and fad dances of the past such as Bunny Hop, Big Apple, and Hokey Pokey are non-partner line dances. If all the non-partner dances from various world cultures were added to this mix we would have to say, without a doubt, that the line dance is the "grand dame of dance!"

LINE DANCE STYLE

The dance reflects the kind of music played. Western line dance steps are precise and have a "calculated look." The feet are close to the floor, and the steps, if traveling, glide. Weight is carried on the balls of the feet accompanied by a slight knee bend for balance. The upper torso is quiet, arms and shoulders relaxed. There is little or no arm movement and high kicks are discouraged.

Achy Breaky

ACHY BREAKY IS A Country Western Line Dance to the song "Achy Breaky Heart." Don Von Tress wrote the song, calling it "Don't Tell My Heart." Unable to remember the title, the audience would request Billy Ray Cyrus to sing that "Achy Breaky" song. Mercury is credited with capitalizing on the country dance craze and packaging a videotape with the *Achy Breaky* line dance when it released a single. The song and dance caught on fast. "Achy Breaky Heart" became a hit and Billy Ray Cyrus won a 1993 American Music Award. This dance was choreographed by Melanie Greenwood.

METER: 4/4. Directions are presented in beats.

MUSIC: "Achy Breaky Heart."

FORMATION: Lines of dancers, all facing front.

DIRECTIONS FOR THE DANCE

■ *Beats*

1–4 Grapevine. Beginning right, step sideward right, cross left behind right, step sideward right, stomp left in place.

5–8 Bump hips left, right, and hold.

9–12 Star. Point right toe back, side, front, turning three-quarters counterclockwise on ball of left foot, step right in place.

13–16 Step backward left, right in place, lift knee up (hitch) turning one-quarter counterclockwise, step left in place.

17–20 Moving backward, step right, left, right, stomp left.

21–24 Bump hips left, right, twice left.

25–26 Step right turning one-quarter clockwise, scuff left forward.

27–28 Step left, pivoting counterclockwise one-half turn, scuff right forward. Now face a new direction.

29–32 Grapevine. Step sideward right, cross left behind right, step right sideward, step left and clap. Now right foot is free to begin grapevine from the beginning. There are two consecutive grapevines in a row (first step and last step of the dance), *both to the right.*

Cowboy Boogie

COWBOY BOOGIE, also called *Country Boogie,* is a Country Western Line Dance.

METER: 4/4. medium to fast. Directions are presented in beats.

MUSIC: "Friends in Low Places," or popular 4/4 Country Western tune.

FORMATION: Scattered, all facing music.

DIRECTIONS FOR THE DANCE

Beats

1–4 Grapevine. Beginning right, step sideward, cross left behind right, step sideward right, scuff left heel forward and clap.

5–8 Repeat grapevine beginning left.

9–10 Step right in place, scuff left heel.

11–12 Step left in place, scuff right heel.

13–16 Moving backwards, step right, left, right, and lift left knee up (hitch).

17–18 Rock forward left, touch right in back.

19–20 Rock backward right, touch left in front.

21–24 Rock forward left, rock back right, rock forward left, pivoting on left foot, one-quarter turn left and swing right knee up (hitch).

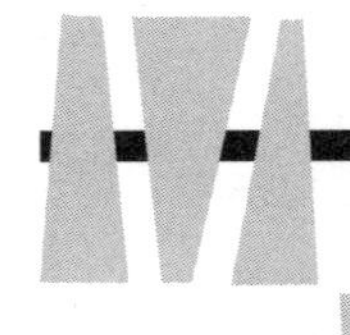

El Tango Sereno*

EL TANGO SERENO (Sair AY no) (Serene) has been composed as a Line Dance by Henry "Buzz" Glass, February 1994. The composer was granted a fellowship to study in Mexico in 1954–55. He also taught Social Dance for a major dance studio in the United States. The dance may be adapted to a "Four Corners" dance, as well as partner or mixer dance.

RECORDS: Hoctor 45—H–640 or other Tangos as El Choclo, La Cumparsita, or Adios Muchachos. See Round Dance labels as Grenn (Top), Windsor or others.

FORMATION: Form lines facing forward. Hands may be gracefully extended sideward. Woman may move skirts to the flow of the dance.

DIRECTIONS FOR THE DANCE

METER: 4/4

Measures

INTRODUCTION

1–4 Wait in place two measures. Step sideward left (count 1), step right in place (count 2), step left next to right (count 3), step right in place (count 4). Repeat the above (4 counts). Note: Adapt to individual introduction.

I POINT AND DRAW, WALK 2 3

1–2 Point left foot sideward (toes down) (count 1), hold (count 2), draw left foot to right (count 3), hold (count 4). Moving sideward left, take 3 walking steps (left, right, left) making a half-turn right on the third step to face right (3 counts) and point right foot down (count 4).

3–4 Repeat action of measures 1–2, beginning right. End making a quarter turn left to face front.

II STEP-TOGETHER CROSS/SIDE BREAK

1 (Like a Twinkle step or Yemenite Three)

Step sideward left (count 1), step right beside left (count 2), step left across right (count 3) and hold (count 4). Maneuver on hold to face front.

2 Step sideward right (count 1), step left beside right (count 2), step right across left (count 3), hold (count 4).

3 Repeat action of part II, measure 1. End facing front, weight on left.

4 Side-Break: Sep sideward right (count 1), step left in place (count 2), step on right beside left (count 3), and hold (count 4).

*El Tango Sereno included by permission of Henry "Buzz" Glass, Oakland, California.

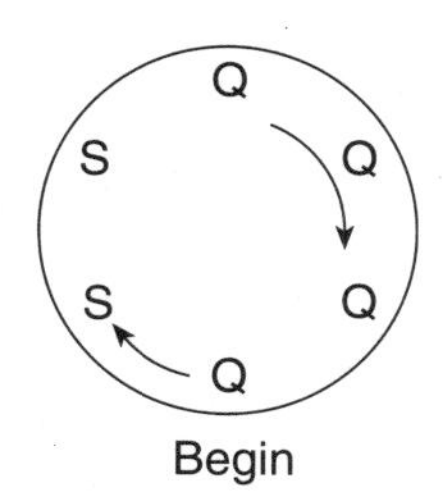

▪ III CLOCKWISE CIRCLE

1 Moving clockwise in a circle (abut 4 feet in diameter) step left diagonally forward (sideward) (count 1) and hold (count 2). Step right forward and in front of left (count 3) and hold (count 4). Slow Slow.

2 Beginning a series of "quick steps," step left on top of circle (count 1), step backward on right (count 2), step back-sideward on left (count 3), step backward on right (count 4). Quick, Quick, Quick, Quick.

3–4 Follow circular pattern, repeating action of Part III, measures 1–2.

▪ IV TEMPTATION TWO-STEP

The Temptation Two-Step has a feeling of "step-close-step" and "down up down" with a gentle thrust of bent elbow.

1 Facing sideward left, step left forward (count 1), bending knees, close right to left straightening (count 2), step left forward bending knees (count 3). Maneuver on both feet making a half-turn right and straightening (count 4) to face right side.

2 Repeat action of Part IV, measure 1 stepping right, left, right and end facing front again.

▪ V GET DOWN STEP

1 Beginning left, take a short step forward (count 1), step right backward in place (count 2), and straightening step left beside right (count 3), step right beside left (count 4).

2 Repeat action of Part V, measure 1.

VARIATION: One may use the Get Down Step to maneuver to face a new wall for the repetition of the dance. This makes it a Four Corners dance.

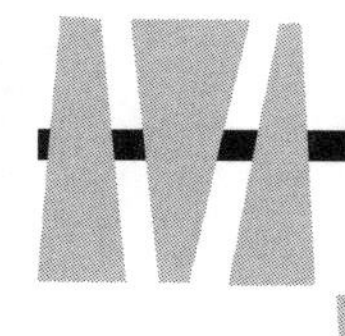

Electric Slide

ELECTRIC SLIDE IS A Country Western Line Dance.

METER: 4/4, medium to fast. Directions are presented in beats.

MUSIC: Any popular 4/4 Country Western tune.

FORMATION: Lines of dancers, all facing front.

DIRECTIONS FOR THE DANCE

▪ *Beats*

1–4 Beginning right, step sideward right, close left to right, step sideward right, close left to right, step touch.

5–8 Repeat same action to left

Electric Slide (continued)

9–12 Moving backward, step right, close left to right, step right and touch left heel to right foot.

13–14 Rock forward left, touch right (dig) in place. May swing right arm in arc, bending over, and touch floor in front of left foot on the "dig."

15–16 Rock backward right, touch left (dig) in place.

17–18 Step left (count one), pivoting on left one-quarter turn left and brush right foot forward (count two).

■ *Variations*

1–4 Take three fast slides to right, letting left foot drag, step right, touch left. Repeat to left.

1–4 Or grapevine right (right, left, right), touch left heel. Repeat left.

STYLE: Bend knees on grapevine.

■ ELECTRIC SLIDE TO FUNK MUSIC

MUSIC: Any popular Funk tune.

STYLE: Bring knees up high. Bend elbows and work arms like a hammer alternately. On the rock, twist shoulders and torso forward and back. Add hops, at every opportunity. Whole body makes exaggerated moves to the music.

Freeze

FREEZE IS A Country Western Line Dance.

METER: 4/4, medium fast. Directions presented in beats.

RECORD: MH 37.

CASSETTE: MH C37.

MUSIC: Suggested tunes: "Tulsa Line," "Swingin'," "Elvira."

FORMATION: Line of dancers, all facing forward.

DIRECTIONS FOR THE DANCE

■ *Beats*

1–4 Grapevine: beginning left, step left sideward; step right behind left; step sidewards left; lift right knee turned out, crossing right heel in front of left, then kick right foot out.

5–8 Grapevine: beginning right, repeat action of measures 1–4 to the right.

9–12 Traveling backward, step back left, right, left; lift right knee turned out, crossing right heel in front of left, then kick right foot out.

13–14 Rock. Step forward right, touch left to right. Step backward left, touch right to left.

15–16 Turning one-quarter turn right, pivot on right foot with left knee bent, foot off the floor, touch left to right. Weight remains on right. Left foot is free.

STYLE: Review Line Dance style, p. 90.

Variations

1. Funky or Hip Hop music. Use upper body and arms, turning shoulders left and right. Lift knees high.
2. Zydeco Music. Upper torso quiet, footwork subtle. Merenque step and body action.

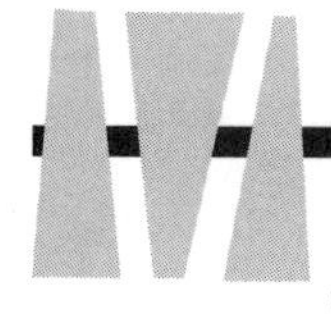

Four Corners

FOUR CORNERS IS A Country Western Line Dance.

METER: 4/4 medium to fast. Directions presented in beats.

RECORD: MH 35.

CASSETTE: MH C35.

MUSIC: Suggested tunes: "Tulsa Line," "Swingin'," "Elvira."

FORMATION: Free formation, all facing music.

DIRECTIONS FOR THE DANCE

Beats

1–2 Swivel heels to left and return.

3–4 Swivel heels to right and return.

5 Touch right heel forward, foot turned out to 45° angle.

6 Sweep right heel in front of left.

7–8 Touch left heel forward, foot turned out to 45° angle, and return. Weight on right.

9 Touch left heel forward, foot turned out to 45° angle.

10 Sweep left heel in front of right.

11 Touch left heel forward, foot turned out to 45° angle.

12 Touch left toe backward.

13–14 Step left forward, chugging with right knee raised.

15 Step backward right.

Four Corners (continued)

16–19	Repeat action of beats 12–15.
20	Touch left toe backward.
21–22	Turning foot slightly left, step left forward, chugging while turning a quarter-turn left with right knee raised.
23–26	Grapevine: step right, crossing in front of left; step left sideward; step right behind left; touch left toe to left side.
27	Return left to right, stepping on left.
28–29	Touch right toe to right side and return right to left. Weight on both feet.

STYLE: Review Line Dance style, p. 90.

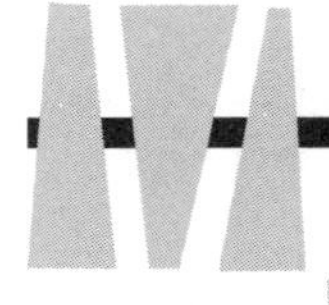

Macarena

MACARENA IS A Latin line dance that appeared in the United States in 1995 and became instantly popular. Macarena, a women's name in Spain, is also the name of a revered virgin in Seville. The song was written by A. R. Monge and R. Ruiz and recorded by Los Del Rio. In 1993 it became a popular hit in Spain.

METER: 4/4. Directions are presented in beats.

MUSIC: "Macarena" by Los Del Rio, Bayside Boys, Los Del Mar.

FORMATION: Solo dance with individuals facing the same direction.

DIRECTIONS FOR THE DANCE

Beats

Beginning right, step alternately right, left in place.

1–2	Extend right arm straight out in front, palm facing down. Repeat with left arm.
3–4	Turn right palm to face up. Turn left palm to face up.
5–6	Place right hand on left inside elbow (left palm is still facing down). Place left hand on right inside elbow. Forearms are now crossed.
7–8	Place right hand back of head. Place left hand back of head.
9–10	Place right hand on left waist. Place left hand on right waist.
11–12	Place right hand on right hip. Place left hand on left hip.
13–14	Swirl hips right, left right.
15–16	Jump turning right a quarter-turn, clap and shout.

STYLE: *Macarena* is a Merenge style dance. Each foot is placed flat and firm on the floor, but the weight is on the ball of the foot for easy balance. The footwork must be disciplined, feet face squarely forward and close together. The step is small. The hip movement is controlled, knee action is as in the Rumba. The shoulders rock slightly sideways with the foot pattern. The body movement is not meant to be exaggerated. The lively music and the character of the step give the dance a delightful touch of humor.

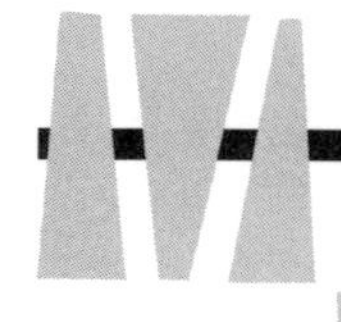

Para Bailar*

PARA BAILAR (IN ORDER to Dance) presents an easy line dance as choreographed by Henry "Buzz" Glass, January 1997. It uses Caribbean rhythms with a dose of Latin patterns to form a delightful dance recalling a deep blue sea and sculptured palm trees with a splash of greenness.

RECORD: Limbo Rock, Challenge #45-9131

FORMATION: Lines of dancers all facing front, may be done "four wall style" or facing front and back wall alternately.

DIRECTIONS FOR THE DANCE

METER: 2/4

Measures

I BEGUINE BASIC/SAMBA BALANCE

1–2 Beguine Basic: stand with feet about a foot apart. Bending slightly forward, step left in place (count 1), leaning sideward left, touch right ball of foot sideward about a foot apart (count and) step left in place (count 2). Now step right directly under body (count 1), lean sideward right and touch left ball of foot left sideward (count and), then step right in place (count 2). There is an easy sway and accent of hip movement.

3–4 Samba Balance: balance forward with a two-step (flat-toe-flat), left, right, left (counts 1 and 2) and then backward, right, left, right (counts 1 and 2).

5–8 Repeat action of measures 1–4.

II CROSS STEP

1–4 With body bent forward, move sideward right with 7 steps crossing left (flat foot) over the ball of right foot with short rapid steps (left, right, left, right, left, right, left) (2 measures). Reverse direction, move sideward left with right (flat) in front of left (2 measures). Movement has the feeling of a buzz step with slight movement in hips and knees.

III TWISTY TWO-STEP

5–8 Accenting movement with the sway of arms at waist level, move forward with twisty two-step (left, right, left) (flat-toe-flat) (counts 1 and 2), then right, left, right (counts 1 and 2). Making a quarter turn left, use the same pattern left, right, left and right, left, right (2 measures) to face a new wall Four Corners.

**Para Bailar* included by permission of Henry "Buzz" Glass, Oakland, California.

Slappin' Leather

Slappin' Leather is a Country Western Line Dance choreographed by Gayle Brandon.

METER: 4/4, medium to fast. Directions presented in beats.

MUSIC: Suggested tunes: "Elvira," "Tulsa Times," "Swingin'," "Baby's Got Her Blue Jeans On."

FORMATION: Line of dancers, all face front.

DIRECTIONS FOR THE DANCE

Beats

1–4 Swivel, weight on balls of feet; spread heels apart, heels together; spread heels apart, heels together.

5–8 Touch right heel forward, step right in place. Touch left heel forward, step left in place.

9–12 Repeat action of beats 5–8.

13–14 Tap right heel in front twice, foot turned out.

15–16 Tap right toe in back twice.

17–20 Star. Touch right toe forward, to right side, behind left, and to right side.

21 Slap leather! Weight remains on left. Swing right foot behind left and slap right boot with left hand.

22 While turning a quarter-turn left (pivot on left foot), swing right foot to right side and slap right boot with right hand.

23 Swing right foot in front of left and slap right boot with left hand.

24 Swing right foot to right side and slap right boot with right hand.

25–28 Grapevine: Beginning right, step right, step left behind right, step sideward right, chug (scoot) right, lifting left knee up (hitch), and clap hands.

29–32 Beginning left, repeat action of beats 23–26 to the left.

33–36 Traveling backward, step right, left, right, chug (scoot) right, lifting left foot behind right leg and slap left heel with right hand.

37–38 Step forward left, close right next to left. Weight on both feet.

39–40 Step forward left, stomp on right foot next to left, weight on both feet.

STYLE: Review Line Dance style p. 90.

Tush Push

TUSH PUSH IS A Country Western Line Dance.

METER: 4/4, medium to fast. Directions presented in beats.

MUSIC: "Two of a Kind" by Garth Brooks or any popular 4/4 Country Western tune.

FORMATION: Scattered, all facing music.

DIRECTIONS FOR THE DANCE

Beats

1–4 Beginning right, lift heel and tap (press) heel four times.

5–8 Beginning left, lift heel and tap (press) heel four times.

9–12 Swivel, heels together, right, left, right, left, clap.

13–14 Bump hips right twice.

15–16 Bump hips left twice.

17–20 In a circular counterclockwise motion, bump hips first to right, circling twice.

21–24 Cha Cha Cha. Beginning right, step forward, close left to right, step forward right (counts one and two), rock forward left, rock back right.

25–28 Moving backward, step left, close right to left, step left (counts one and two) rock back right, rock forward left.

29–32 Repeat Cha Cha Cha. Step right forward, close left to right, step forward right, step left forward, pivoting one-half turn counterclockwise, step right in place. Now facing opposite direction.

33–36 Moving forward, step left, close right to left, step left (counts one and two), step right forward pivoting one-half turn counterclockwise, step left in place.

37–40 Step forward right pivoting one-quarter turn counter-clockwise, step left in place, stamp right next to left, clap.

Watermelon Crawl*

WATERMELON CRAWL IS A line dance choreographed by Sue Lipscomb.

METER: 4/4. Directions are presented in beats. (40 beats)

MUSIC: "Watermelon Crawl" Tracy Byrd, Atlantic.

FORMATION: Line of dancers all facing front.

DIRECTIONS FOR THE DANCE

■ *Beats*

1–2 Beginning right, touch right toe to left toe, pointing right toe and knee diagonally left. Touch right heel to left toe, pointing right toe and knee diagonally right.

3–4 Step right beside left (beat 3), step left beside right (ball of foot) (beat and), step right beside left (beat 4).

5–6 Touch left toe beside right toe, pointing left toe and knee diagonally right, touch left heel beside right toe, pointing left toe and knee diagonally left.

7–8 Step left beside right, step right beside left (ball of foot) (beat and), step left beside right.

9–10 Charleston: beginning right, step forward right, kick left foot forward and clap (all kicks are about 4 to 6 inches high).

11–12 Step back left, touch right toe back and clap.

13–14 Repeat action of beats 11–12.

15–16 Step back left, touch ball of right foot beside left and clap.

17–18 Grapevine: beginning right, step side right, step left behind right.

19–20 Step right side, kick left foot forward diagonally right.

21–22 Step left side, cross right foot behind left.

23–24 Step left side, pivoting one-quarter turn left, touch ball of right foot beside left foot and clap.

25 Take a long step forward right (both knees bent).

26–27 Slide left foot forward towards right foot, continuous motion (2 beats) ending left beside right.

28 Straighten up and clap (weight remains on right foot).

29 Take long step back left (both knees bent).

**Watermelon Crawl* included by permission of Sue Lipscomb, Chicago, IL.

30–31 Slide right foot back to left foot, continuous motion (2 beats) ending right beside left.

32 Shift weight to left foot, straighten up and clap.

33–34 Raise left heel as weight shifts to right foot and push right hip to right side (beat 33) (right leg straight, left knee bent). Raise right heel as weight shifts to left foot and push left hip to left side (beat 34) (left leg straight, right knee bent).

35–36 Repeat action of beats 33–34.

37–38 Step forward right (beat 37) (left leg extended back with left toe touching floor), turn counterclockwise one-half turn (beat and), shift weight forward to left foot (beat 38).

39–40 Repeat action of beats 37 and 38.

Western Wind*

WESTERN WIND IS A Country Western Line Dance choreographed by Kathy Du Bois, La Crosse, Wisconsin in 1995.

METER: 4/4. Directions presented in beats.

MUSIC: "Any Way the Wind Blows" by Brother Phelps.

FORMATION: Lines of dancers, all facing front.

DIRECTIONS FOR THE DANCE

Beats

ROCK AND CROSS

1–2 Beginning right, rock onto right to right side, rock onto left in place.

3–4 Step right across in front of left, hold.

5–6 Rock onto left to left side, rock onto right in place.

7–8 Step left across in front of right, hold.

STAMP, CLAP

1–2 Stamp forward right, clap

3–4 Stamp forward left, clap

5 Stamp forward right (weight remains on left)

6–7 Clap, clap, hold.

8 Hold.

**Western Wind* included by permission of Kathy DuBois of La Crosse, Wisconsin, 1995

Western Wind (continued)

▪ HIPS RIGHT, LEFT

1–2 Shift weight to right foot and bump hips right twice.

3–4 Shift weight to left foot and bump hips left twice.

5–6 Step forward right, turning one-quarter counterclockwise, step left in place.

7–8 Step forward right, turning one-quarter counterclockwise, step left in place.

▪ STEP, SCUFF, HITCH

1–2 Step forward right, scuff left.

3–4 Hitch left knee scooting forward on right, step forward left.

5–6 Hook right foot behind left ankle, turn one-quarter counterclockwise (weight on left).

7–8 Stamp right next to left twice (weight on left).

▪ GRAPEVINE

1–2 Step right to right side, step left behind right.

3–4 Step right to right side touch left next to right turning one-quarter counterclockwise.

5–6 Step left to left side, step right behind left.

7–8 Step left to left side, scuff right foot, turning one-quarter counterclockwise.

▪ GRAPEVINE

1–8 Repeat action, Grapevine 1–8.

5 Latin Dances

Cha Cha Cha

A CUBAN INNOVATION OF the old basic Latin form (danson), the *Cha Cha Cha* is said to be a combination of the Mambo and American Swing. A close look shows its rhythm to be that of a Triple Mambo, its style that of the Rumba, and its open swingy variations that of the Triple Lindy. It does not have as heavy a quality or as large a foot pattern as the Mambo; nor has it the smooth sophistication or the conservative figures of the Rumba. It reflects a light, breezy mood, a carefree gaiety, and a trend, in the challenge steps, for dancers to ad-lib variations to their heart's content. Consequently one sees variations in almost every known position.

CHA CHA CHA RHYTHM

In 4/4 time, the catchy rhythm and delightful music of the Cha Cha Cha have brought dancers and musicians alike a new treat in the undeniably Latin flavor. The rhythm has been a controversy. Originally it was done on the offbeat of the measure, and then there was a widespread acceptance of the onbeat rhythm, which is the easier way, but again the trend is to go back to the offbeat rhythm. Analysis in this edition will be done with the offbeat rhythm.

4/4	/	S	S	Q Q	/ S			
		2	3	4 and	1			

uneven rhythm

The rhythm is an uneven beat pattern of slow slow quick quick slow and will be counted 2 3 4 *and* 1, with the 4 *and* 1 being the familiar Cha Cha Cha triple. Rhythmically the beats are as follows:

4/4 | — ♩ ♩ ♪ ♪ | ♩

cha cha cha

Note that the last beat of the triple is a quarter note, not an eighth note as is sometimes misinterpreted.

CHA CHA CHA STYLE

The Cha Cha Cha is seen danced in a variety of positions as it moves in and out of the variations. However, the three basic positions are closed position, face-to-face position, and challenge position (which is completely apart from but facing partner). Beginners like the facing position with two hands joined. The woman holds her arms up with the elbows just in front of her body. The hands are up, fingers pointing inward. The man reaches over the top of the woman's forefingers and grasps her fingers with his fingers and thumb. The woman exerts a little resistance against his fingers. Both man and woman hold the forearms firm so that the man can push, pull, or turn her, and she responds, not with arm motion or shoulder rotation, but with body motion forward, back, or turning. The arm and hand, when free, are **held up parallel to the floor in bent-arm position** and they turn with the body as it moves.

The Cha Cha Cha, with its light bouncy quality, is delightfully Latin as it carries with it some of the subtleness of the Rumba movement. The forward foot should be placed nearly flat on the floor. The knee is bent over the stepping foot. The back step (instead of a flat step that tends to give the appearance of a sag) is a toe step, holding the body firmly so as to avoid the sag. The Cha Cha Cha triple is taken with very small steps in place or traveling but is kept close to the floor. The upper body is held comfortably upright and the head focuses on one's partner in a typical gracious Latin manner. The eye contact brings the dance to life.

FUNDAMENTAL CHA CHA CHA STEPS

Directions are for man, facing line of direction; lady's part is reverse, except as noted.

■ BACK BASIC STEP

(Challenge or Two hands joined)

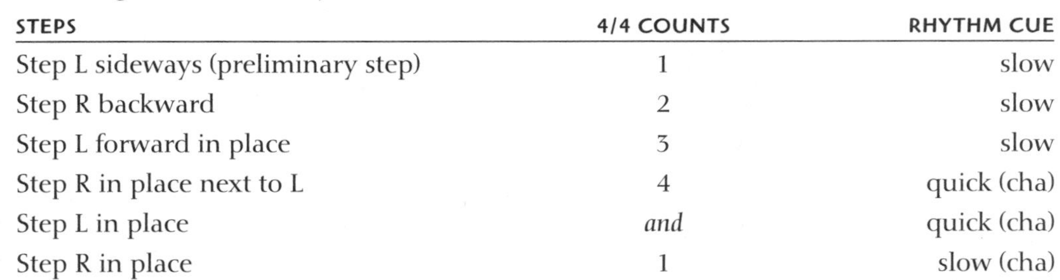

STEPS	4/4 COUNTS	RHYTHM CUE
Step L sideways (preliminary step)	1	slow
Step R backward	2	slow
Step L forward in place	3	slow
Step R in place next to L	4	quick (cha)
Step L in place	*and*	quick (cha)
Step R in place	1	slow (cha)

NOTE: There is a side step on the accented first beat to begin the dance only and it is not used again.

■ FORWARD BASIC STEP

STEPS	4/4 COUNTS	RHYTHM CUE
Step L forward	2	slow
Step R back in place	3	slow
Step L in place next to R	4	quick (cha)
Step R in place	*and*	quick (cha)
Step L in place	1	slow (cha)

STEP CUE: Back forward Cha Cha Cha/forward back Cha Cha Cha.

STYLE: The back basic has the toe step, the forward basic has the flat style (see Cha Cha Cha style). Dancers have a tendency to pound the feet on the floor for the Cha Cha Cha. It should be neither a pounding nor scuffing sound.

LEAD: The man leads by pulling with his right hand going into the back basic or pushing with the left hand going into the forward basic. If arm and elbow are firm, finger resistance aids in getting the message across. The body should respond by moving backward or forward.

POSITION: The basic Cha Cha Cha may be done in closed, facing, or challenge position.

NOTE: This is the basic step of Cha Cha Cha. The forward half is also called the "forward break"; the back half is the "back break." They may be used with either foot leading when called for in a particular variation. Sometimes the Cha Cha Cha part of the step is used to travel rather than being in place.

■ *Cha Cha Cha Step Variations*

- Open Break
- Cross Over
- Cross Over Turn
- Chase Half-Turn
- Full Turn
- Jody Break
  - Reverse Jody
  - Shadow
- Kick Swivel
- Kick Freeze

■ OPEN BREAK

(Two hands joined or Closed position)

The purpose of the break is to change position from face to face to side by side. The couple may open to either right or left. The right break is described next.

Fundamental Cha Cha Cha Steps (continued)

■ RIGHT BREAK

STEPS	4/4 COUNTS	RHYTHM CUE
Step R backward, releasing R hand hold with woman	2	slow
Step L forward in place	3	slow
Step R in place, turning one-quarter clockwise to face R in a side-by-side position	4	quick
Step L in place	*and*	quick
Step R in place	1	slow

STEP CUE: Break open turn Cha Cha Cha.

STYLE: The released hand and arm remain up in place and turn with the body.

LEAD: The man releases right hand or right turn, let hand for left turn, and guides through to the side-by-side position with the other joined hand. As the man does this, the woman should exert slight resistance against his arm with her arm or wrist to facilitate following forthcoming leads in side-by-side position.

NOTE: The left break will start forward with the left foot and turn one-quarter left.

■ CROSS OVER

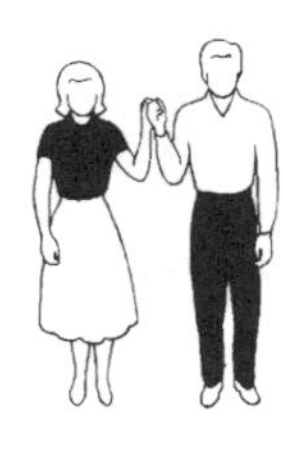

(Side-by-side position, having taken the open break to the right)

Man's left is holding woman's right hand. Start with the inside foot (man's left, woman's right).

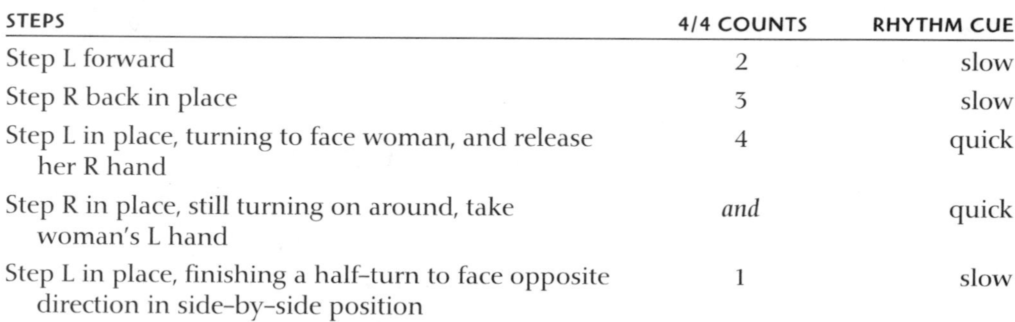

STEPS	4/4 COUNTS	RHYTHM CUE
Step L forward	2	slow
Step R back in place	3	slow
Step L in place, turning to face woman, and release her R hand	4	quick
Step R in place, still turning on around, take woman's L hand	*and*	quick
Step L in place, finishing a half-turn to face opposite direction in side-by-side position	1	slow

Repeat, starting with the inside foot (man's right, woman's left) and turning back to starting position.

STEP CUE: Forward turn Cha Cha Cha.

STYLE: On the forward step, the inside foot should step straight ahead. The body is upright and the head is looking over the inside shoulder at partner. The free hand is up. Avoid bouncing, leaning forward, turning back on partner, or looking at the floor.

LEAD: The man's inside hand guides forward into the forward step and pulls back to start the turn. If the arms of both man and woman remain up when turning, the arms are ready to receive the lead when changing from one hand to the other.

NOTE: If the open break was taken to the left side, then the cross over step will begin with the inside foot (man's right, woman's left). The cross over step may be repeated from side to side any number of times.

▪ RETURN TO BASIC

(Side-by-side position, facing right starting with the inside foot)

STEPS	4/4 COUNTS	RHYTHM CUE
Step L forward	2	slow
Step R backward in place, turning to face partner	3	slow
Step L, R, L in place taking both of the woman's hands	4 *and* 1	quick quick slow
With R foot now free, go into a back basic		

▪ RETURN TO BASIC

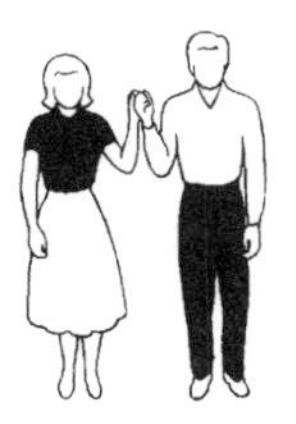

(Side-by-side position, facing left starting with the inside foot)

STEPS	4/4 COUNTS	RHYTHM CUE
Step R forward	2	sow
Step L backward in place, turning to face partner	3	slow
Step R, L, R, in place taking both of the woman's hands	4 *and* 1	quick quick slow
With the L foot now free, go into a forward basic		

LEAD: If the man uses pressure against the woman's fingers of the hand he holds just before he takes both hands, she will recognize the intent to go back to basic and will facilitate the transition.

▪ CROSS OVER TURN

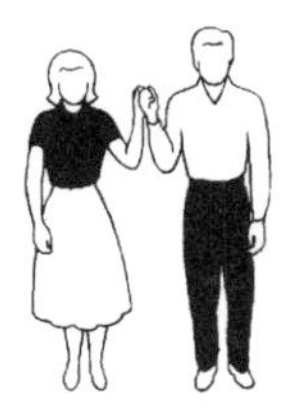

(Side by side, facing left, starting with the inside foot [man's right, woman's left])

STEPS	4/4 COUNTS	RHYTHM CUE
Step R forward, turning counterclockwise away from the woman about halfway around	2	slow
Step L in place, continuing to turn counterclockwise, completing the turn around to face the woman	3	slow
Bring feet together and hold	4 *and* 1	quick quick slow
Free the L foot and step into a forward basic on count 2		

STEP CUE: Out around *hold* Cha Cha Cha/forward step Cha Cha Cha.

STYLE: A smooth spin on the ball of the foot is taken on counts 2 and 3 and then a sudden hold during the Cha Cha Cha part gives this variation a bit of special pizazz. It is necessary to count the timing carefully so as to step forward into basic again on count 2. The lady is turning clockwise.

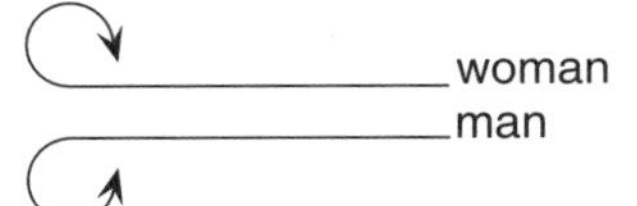

LEAD: The man, knowing he is going into the cross over turn, will not grasp the woman's hand as he comes through from the other side but will place the heel of his hand against the back of her hand and push out slightly into the turn. He must then direct her into a back basic as he steps into his forward basic.

NOTE: Of course, the turn may be taken from either side. The man may use this variation as a lead into challenge position, in which case he will not rejoin hands with partner but will remain apart, facing partner.

▪ CHASE HALF-TURN

(Challenge position or Two hands joined)

It is a turning figure in which the man is always one turn ahead of the woman. He will start the turn while she takes a back basic. On her next forward basic she starts the turn. After the desired number of turns he will finish with a forward basic while she completes her last turn to face him. The forward break is used with alternating feet for all turns.

Fundamental Cha Cha Cha Steps (continued)

STEPS	4/4 COUNTS	RHYTHM CUE
Man's Part		
Step L forward, turning clockwise on both feet halfway around with back to woman	2	slow
Take weight on R foot	3	slow
Step L, R, L in place	4 *and* 1	quick quick slow
Step R forward, turning counterclockwise a half-turn, on both feet, to face woman's back	2	slow
Take weight on L foot	3	slow
Step R, L, R in place	4 *and* 1	quick quick slow
Woman's Part		
Step R backward	2	slow
Step L forward in place	3	slow
Step R, L, R in place	4 *and* 1	quick quick slow
Step L forward, turning clockwise on both feet halfway around with back to man	2	slow
Take weight on R foot	3	slow
Step L, R, L in place	4 *and* 1	quick quick slow

STEP CUE: Turn about Cha Cha Cha.

STYLE: The turn about is called a swivel turn and is done with both feet in an apart position. The step is forward, the swivel turns toward the back foot, with the weight on the balls of the feet. There is a cocky manner as man and woman look over the shoulder at partner.

LEAD: The man drops both hands when stepping forward left foot, and the rest is a visual lead for the woman. She keeps turning if he does. When the man wishes to go back to basic, he will take a forward basic while she does her last turn and then rejoin hands and go into a back basic on the right foot.

NOTE: The half-turn may be done again and again. A familiar styling is to tap partner's shoulder when facing partner's back.

▪ FULL TURN

(Challenge position)

Step L forward, pivoting clockwise a half-turn. Step right in place, again pivoting clockwise a half-turn. Take Cha Cha Cha in place, facing partner.

LEAD: The lead is a visual one, having let go of hands to start the turn and taking the hands to finish it.

STYLE: The manner is a bit cocky as each looks over the shoulder at partner. The pivoting steps are small and on the ball of the foot for good balance and smoothness.

NOTE: The man will make a complete turn while she does a back basic, and then she follows with a complete turn while he does a back basic.

▪ JODY BREAK

(Two hands joined)

STEPS	4/4 COUNTS	RHYTHM CUE
Step L backward, and at the same time changing hands from a two-hand grasp to a right-hand grasp	2	slow
Step R forward, and at the same time pull with the R hand to guide the woman into a counterclockwise turn	3	slow

Take Cha Cha Cha (L, R, L) in place, guiding the woman into Varsouvienne position (see p. 9) beside the man	4 *and* 1	quick quick slow
Step R backward in Varsouvienne position	2	slow
Step L forward in place and, at the same time, release the left hand and guide the woman with the R hand to turn clockwise	3	slow
Take Cha Cha Cha (R, L, R) in place, guiding the woman back out to original position, facing man completing half-turn clockwise	4 *and* 1	quick quick slow

NOTE: This may be repeated over and over without changing the right-hand grasp. When the man desires to go back to regular basic, he will change to two-hand grasp and forward basic when the woman returns to facing position.

Woman's Part: Starting right foot into regular back break.

Step R backward, allowing man to change from two-hand grasp to a R-hand grasp	2	slow
Step L forward, toeing out and pivoting on L counterclockwise, being guided by man's lead toward Varsouvienne position	3	slow
Take Cha Cha Cha (R, L, R), finishing the turn into Varsouvienne position beside the man	4 *and* 1	quick quick slow
Step L backward in Varsouvienne position	2	slow
Step R forward, toeing out and pivoting on the R clockwise, being guided by the man's lead towards the original facing position	3	slow
Take Cha Cha Cha (L, R, L) in place finishing the turn to face partner	4 *and* 1	quick quick slow

STEP CUE: Back forward Cha Cha Cha.

STYLE: Both man and woman should keep steps small and not get too far apart. Large steps and big movement spoil the beauty of this lovely figure and make it awkward to maneuver.

LEAD: Arm tension control makes it possible for the man's lead to guide the woman smoothly in and out of Varsouvienne position.

■ VARIATIONS FROM JODY POSITION

(Also called Varsouvienne position)

1. **Reverse Jody:** While in Varsouvienne position, both break back on the inside foot, and while stepping forward turn one-half clockwise in place to reverse Varsouvienne, with the woman on the left of the man, and take Cha Cha Cha in place. Repeat, starting with the inside foot, and turn counterclockwise to end up in original position. This may be repeated any number of times. Steps are very small. Both partners are using back break continuously.
2. **Shadow:** While in Varsouvienne position, both break on the inside foot, then releasing the Varsouvienne grasp, step forward, the man guiding the woman across in front of him. Take the Cha Cha Cha, finishing the cross over, and catch inside hands. Woman is to left of man. Repeat, starting with the inside foot and crossing the woman in front of the man to a hand-grasp position on his right. This may be repeated any number of times. Return to Varsouvienne position with the woman on the right when ready to go back to a facing position and back to a regular basic.

Fundamental Cha Cha Cha Steps (continued)

STYLE: In the shadow, couples do not get farther apart than a bent-elbow control. The footwork in the apart position changes on count 2 to a back-cross style; that is, the inside foot crosses behind the standing foot. The action of the changing sides with partner is done on the Cha Cha Cha beats like a running motion.

STEP CUE: Cross step Cha Cha Cha.

LEAD: The man leads with his fingers, pulling her on count 4.

NOTE: The man may lead the woman across in front of him or in back of him.

▪ KICK SWIVEL

(Two hands joined)

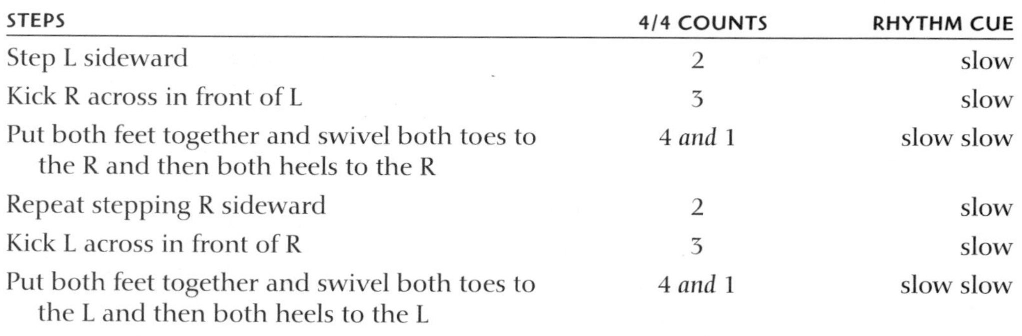

STEPS	4/4 COUNTS	RHYTHM CUE
Step L sideward	2	slow
Kick R across in front of L	3	slow
Put both feet together and swivel both toes to the R and then both heels to the R	4 *and* 1	slow slow
Repeat stepping R sideward	2	slow
Kick L across in front of R	3	slow
Put both feet together and swivel both toes to the L and then both heels to the L	4 *and* 1	slow slow
Return to basic from either side by using the free foot, if left to lead a forward basic, if right to lead a back basic.		

STEP CUE: Step kick swivel swivel.

STYLE: Dancers should take small steps. Keep the kick low and take the swivel steps with the feet and knees close together. One may bend the knees slightly. The man and woman kick in the same direction.

LEAD: The man pulls both of the woman's hands in the direction of the step kick, and then he puts the hands close together and gives a push-pull action for the swivel. Part of the lead the woman picks up visually.

NOTE: The two swivel steps take the place of the three cha cha cha steps and are even rhythm, being the equivalent of counts 4 and 1.

▪ KICK FREEZE

(Facing position or Closed position)

STEPS	4/4 COUNTS	RHYTHM CUE
Step L sideward	2	slow
Kick R across in front of L	3	slow
Touch R foot sideward to the R in a stride position (no weight change); count 4—hold count 1	4, 1	slow slow
Step R, L, R, moving to the R without changing position	2 *and* 3	quick quick slow
Repeat on the same foot	4, 1, 2, 3, 4, *and* 1	

STEP CUE: The posture on the freeze straightens to be extra firm and holds with the leg extended sideward. Arms extend sideward to butterfly position. The body may turn slightly to the right during the Cha Cha Cha but should end up facing partner.

LEAD: The man pulls both of the woman's hands in the direction of the kick and then suddenly increases tension as arms and legs swing to freeze position. They hold the position 1 beat. Then he releases pressure and leads sideward for the quick slow beats.

NOTE: The freeze is on counts 4, 1. These are two extra counts added to the regular pattern. It is best to take the kick freeze twice in order to make it fit rhythmically with the music. Return to basic by leading into a back basic with the right foot.

CHA CHA CHA COMBOS

The Cha Cha Cha routines are combinations for practice, listed from simple to complex. (Partners facing, unless otherwise indicated.)

1. *Open Break and Cross Over*
   2 forward and back basics with open break
   4 cross overs
2. *Cross Over With Turn*
   2 basics with open break
   3 cross overs and turn
   repeat
3. *Cross Over and Freeze*
   2 basics with open break
   2 cross overs
   2 freeze
   1 cross over and turn
4. *Basic and Chase*
   2 basics
   4 half turns
   2 full turns
5. *Basic and Jody*
   2 basics
   4 jody breaks
6. *Jody Variations*
   2 basics
   jody break
   2 double jody
   2 shadow
7. *Basic and Kick Freeze*
   2 basics (closed position)
   2 kick freeze

Mambo

THE *MAMBO* IS A CUBAN DANCE that appeared on the ballroom scene in the United States shortly after World War II. It is a very free dance allowing for individual interpretation and innovation. Probably due to its difficult rhythm, it became less popular in the 1950s than the Cha Cha Cha. However, it did survive and finds renewed interest among dancers in the United States, especially the advanced dancer. Over the years it has become more sophisticated and conservative. It is most often done in closed position.

MAMBO RHYTHM

The rhythm is difficult and has spurred controversy as to whether the rhythm is off-beat or on-beat, that is, quick, quick slow or slow quick quick. Because of its highly syncopated beat, it has been a difficult rhythm to learn. The rhythm pattern described here will be in 4/4 time, that is, quick quick, slow.

4/4 ____ ____ ____ ____
4 1 2 Hold

A preparation step on the first two beats of the measure is helpful in getting started with the Mambo beat.

4/4 ____ ____ ____ ____ ____ ____ ____
1 2 Hold 4 1 2 Hold
Preparation Mambo Rhythm

Mambo (continued)

MAMBO STYLE

The sultry rhythm and oddly accented beat gives the dance a heavy jerky quality, which may be interestingly thought of as a "charge." Basically, the style is Rumba movement, but as one steps forward on the accented 4th beat, it is with the suddenness of a quick lunge, but immediately pulling back for the second quick beat, giving the jerky quality to the dance. The "charge" movement is further accented by a slightly heavier step and the action of the shoulders, which move forward alternately in opposition to the stepping foot. The arms and hands are carried in a bent elbow position parallel to the floor, palms down. The arms move the shoulders and thus the Mambo presents a more dynamic body movement than any of the other Cuban dances.

FUNDAMENTAL MAMBO STEPS

Only the basic step will be given here since all variations may be taken from the Cha Cha Cha. The relationship between the Mambo and the Cha Cha Cha will also be noted. Cha Cha Cha variations may be found on pages 105–110. Directions are for the man, facing the line of direction; woman's part is reverse, except as noted.

Preparation Step (Used only at the beginning of the dance to get started on the Mambo beat)

STEPS	4/4 COUNTS	RHYTHM CUE
Step L in place	1	Quick
Step R in place	2	Quick
Hold	3	Hold
THE BASIC STEP		
Step L diagonally forward to R	4	Quick
Step R back in place	1	Quick
Step L sideward L	2	Slow
Hold, closing R to L	3	No weight change
Step R diagonally backward to L	4	Quick
Step L back in place	1	Quick
Step R sideward R	2	Slow
Hold closing L to R	3	No weight change

STEP CUE: Cross back side, cross back side.

STYLE: Dancers should avoid taking too large a step. The sideward step tends to increase the size of the total pattern and may look very awkward if taken too wide. The quality is sultry.

LEAD: The man's lead is a sharp shoulder action as his shoulder moves forward in opposition to the stepping foot. The woman should merely follow the action of his leading shoulder and not try to figure out which shoulder to move.

POSITION: Closed Position

NOTE: The first half of this step is referred to as the "forward break" and the back half as the "back break." It may be used as in the Cha Cha Cha.

■ *Mambo Variations*

These variations are fully described in the Cha Cha Cha found on pages 105–109. Also refer to Cha Cha Cha Combos on page 111.

Open Break	Cross Over and Cross Turn
Chasse	Jody Break and Double Jody
Shadow	

NOTE: In making the transition from Cha Cha Cha to Mambo one must keep in mind the relationship between the two rhythms.

	Mambo					Cha Cha Cha				
4/4	/				4/4	/		/		
	4	1	2	Hold		1	2	Cha	Cha	Cha

Merengue

THIS CLEVER LITTLE DANCE from the Caribbean could very well be a favorite with the young adult set if they really had a chance to explore it. The music is a peppy, pert, marchlike rhythm, and the dance patterns are the most simple of all the Latin dances. There are two styles: the original "limp step" from the Dominican Republic and the more even, smooth Haitian style. The Haitian style will be described here.

MERENGUE RHYTHM

In 4/4 time, there is a very pronounced beat of the music, which has an exciting uneven beat in the rhythm pattern, but the dance follows the basic beats of the measure and is in even rhythm.

4/4	/ Q	Q	Q	Q
	1	2	3	4

even rhythm

MERENGUE STYLE

Perhaps merengue style could be described as a combination of the rumba movement and a majorette swagger step. The feet are placed flat, but the *weight is on the ball of the foot for easy balance.* It is a controlled hip movement resulting from the bent-knee action

Merengue (continued)

with each step as in the rumba, but it has the almost sassy quality and breezy manner of the majorette. A slight rock sideways with the shoulders to accompany the foot pattern is optional. It is not meant to be an exaggerated body movement, but the lively music and the character of the step give this dance a delightful touch of humor.

With a simple step, the footwork must be disciplined or it may look sloppy. The feet face squarely forward and close tightly together. The step is small.

FUNDAMENTAL MERENGUE STEPS

Directions are for the man; woman's part is reversed, except as noted.

▪ BASIC SIDE STEP

(Closed position)

STEPS	4/4 COUNTS	RHYTHM CUE
Step L sideward	1	quick
Close R to L, take weight on R	2	quick
Step L sideward	3	quick
Close R to L, take weight on R	4	quick

STEP CUE: Side close.

STYLE: Steps are small, head high, focus on partner. Rock body left, right with the step.

LEAD: To lead a sideward moving pattern in closed position, the man should use pressure of the right hand to the left or right to indicate the desired direction.

NOTE: Could travel sideways any number of side steps. Should travel in line of direction.

▪ BOX STEP

(Closed position)

STEPS	4/4 COUNTS	RHYTHM CUE
Step L forward	1	quick
Close R to L, take weight on R	2	quick
Step L backward	3	quick
Close R to L, take weight on R	4	quick

STEP CUE: Forward together back together.

STYLE: The same foot leads each time. The shoulders lead the rock from side to side.

LEAD: To lead a box step the man should use a forward body action followed by right-hand pressure and right elbow pull to the right to take the woman into the forward sequence of the box. Forward pressure of the right hand followed by pressure to the left side takes the woman into the back sequence of the box.

▪ BOX TURN

(Closed position)

STEPS	4/4 COUNTS	RHYTHM CUE
Step L, toeing out to a L one-quarter turn counterclockwise	1	quick
Close R to L, take weight on R	2	quick
Step L backward	3	quick
Close R to L, take weight on R	4	quick

STEP CUE: Turn close back close.

STYLE: A shoulder rock on the turn makes it very easy to lead.

LEAD: See lead indication 6, p. 10.

NOTE: Repeat three times to make a full turn.

■ CROSS STEP

(Closed position)

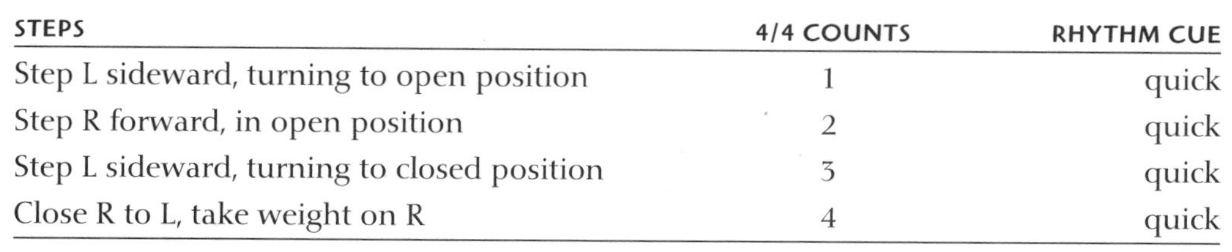

STEPS	4/4 COUNTS	RHYTHM CUE
Step L sideward, turning to open position	1	quick
Step R forward, in open position	2	quick
Step L sideward, turning to closed position	3	quick
Close R to L, take weight on R	4	quick

STEP CUE: Open step side close.

STYLE: Each step must be precisely taken in the closed or open position. If the footwork is not square with each position, the merengue loses all of its distinctive character.

LEAD: To lead into an open position or conversation position, the man should use pressure with the heel of the right hand to turn the woman into open position. The right elbow lowers to the side. The man must simultaneously turn his own body, not just the woman, so that they end facing the same direction. The left arm relaxes slightly and the left hand sometimes gives the lead for steps in the open position.

LEAD: To lead from open to closed position the man should use pressure of the right hand and raise the right arm up to standard position to move the woman into closed position. The woman should not have to be pushed but should swing easily into closed position as she feels the arm lifting. She should move completely around to face the man squarely.

VARIATION: The flick is like the cross step, except that there is a *leap* onto the left foot in open position, bending the right knee and flipping the right foot quickly up in back, and then right foot steps forward and side close as above. The man raises his right elbow as he turns to open position into the leap.

■ SWIVEL

(Open and closed traveling in line of direction)

STEPS	4/4 COUNTS	RHYTHM CUE
Leap L forward in open position flick R foot	1	quick
Step R forward in open position	2	quick
Pivot on R foot to face partner, bringing L foot alongside of R, shift weight to L	3	quick
Pivot on L foot to open position, bringing R foot alongside of L, shift weight to R	4	quick
Repeat pivot on R	1	quick
Repeat pivot on L	2	quick
Step L, turning to closed position	3	quick
Close R to L, taking weight R	4	quick

STEP CUE: Leap step, swivel, swivel, swivel, swivel, side close.

STYLE: Steps are tiny and neat, turning exactly a quarter-turn each time. The body turns with the foot.

Fundamental Merengue Steps (continued)

LEAD: To lead into an open position or conversation position, the man should use pressure with the heel of the right hand to turn the woman into open position. The right elbow lowers to the side. The man must simultaneously turn his own body, not just the woman, so that they end facing the same direction.The left arm relaxes slightly and the left hand sometimes gives the lead for steps in the open position.

LEAD: To lead from open to closed position the man should use pressure of the right hand and raise the right arm up to standard position to move the woman into closed position. The woman should not have to be pushed but should swing easily into closed position as she feels the arm lifting. She should move completely around to face the man squarely.

▪ LADDER

(Closed position)

STEPS	4/4 COUNTS	RHYTHM CUE
Step L sideward	1	quick
Close R to L, take weight on R	2	quick
Step L forward	3	quick
Close R to L, take weight on R	4	quick

STEP CUE: Side close forward close.

STYLE: Footwork small and neat. Face partner squarely.

LEAD: Moving squarely into position helps lead the body. Since there are a lot of direction changes in the merengue, the woman must be extremely alert to the action of his right arm and shoulder.

▪ SIDE CLOSE AND BACK BREAK

(Closed position)

STEPS	4/4 COUNTS	RHYTHM CUE
Step L sideward	1	quick
Close R to L, take weight on R	2	quick
Step L sideward	3	quick
Close R to L, take weight on R	4	quick
Step L sideward	1	quick
Step R, in place, turning to open position	2	quick
Step L backward, in open position	3	quick
Step R, in place, turning to closed position	4	quick

STEP CUE: Side close side close side open back step.

STYLE: There is a rather sudden swing to open position on count 2 of the second measure and then immediately back to closed position on count 4.

LEAD: Man uses his left hand to push woman out quickly to open position.

MERENGUE COMBOS

1. 4 basic steps
   4 box steps
   4 basic steps
   4 box turns
2. 4 basic steps
   4 cross steps
   8 box steps
3. 4 basic steps
   4 box turns
   4 swivels
4. 4 basic steps
   4 ladder
   4 box turns
   4 side close and back break

Rumba

THE LATIN AMERICAN dances are to American dancing what garlic is to the good cook. Used sparingly, they can add a tangy interest to our dancing. The *Rumba* is a Cuban dance (along with the Mambo, Bolero, and Cha Cha Cha) but it has enjoyed greater popularity than any of the others, probably because of its slower, more relaxed, smoother style. The music is usually identified by the tantalizing rhythms of the percussion instruments known as the maracas, which carry the continuous quick beat, and the sticks or bongo drum, which beat out the accented rhythm of the dance.

RUMBA RHYTHM

The Rumba is written in 4/4 time and is played both fast and slow. Many Americans prefer the slower Bolero-type tempo, but actually in the Latin American countries the rumba is danced considerably faster. The rhythm is tricky as it is a 1 2 3, 1 2 3, 1 2 count in 4/4 time.

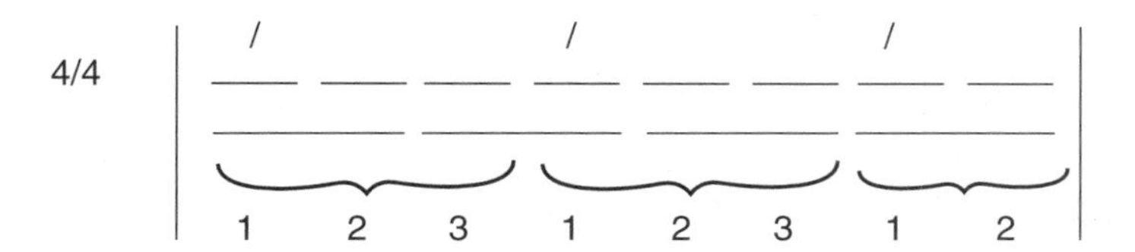

It was taught in the United States for many years as a quick quick slow rhythm, but it has gradually shifted over to a slow quick quick beat with the accent on the first and third beats of the measure. This is the rhythm that will be used in this text.

4/4 S Q Q

1–2 3 4

uneven rhythm

Rumba music has a subtle, beautiful melody with a rolling quality that requires the subtle rolling Rumba movement. It is seldom mistaken for the Cha Cha Cha or mambo music because of its smoothness and continuity.

RUMBA STYLE

Naturally, in the transition, the Rumba lost a lot of its original character. The style has been greatly exaggerated and distorted at times. Some people dance it like the Foxtrot, without attempting to get any of the Cuban flavor. It is hoped that dancers will feel

Rumba (continued)

sufficiently challenged to put in a little extra time in order to get the feeling of the subtle, continuous, rolling motion. Three characteristics make it different from other dances:

1. The action is in the feet and the knees.
2. There is a delayed shift of weight.
3. The upper body is upright and quiet, with a focus on one's partner.

The step itself is comparatively short and flat-footed, with the knee leading. The weight tends to be maintained over the heel of the foot more than in any other dance. The Cuban Rumba movement is a springlike action, resulting from placing the left foot on the floor first, without taking weight but with a bent knee. This is followed by pressing the weight into the floor and straightening the left knee. Accompanying this press into the floor there is a smooth roll of the weight being shifted to that left foot. The right knee begins to bend and leads the right foot, then free of weight, into its new position. The roll is completed as the weight is transferred gradually to the newly placed right foot. Then the entire action is repeated by pressing the weight into the right foot and straightening the right knee rolling smoothly. As the left foot is freed of weight, the knee leads, shifting the left foot to its new position with the weight coming over it, completing the roll.

The knees should be bent directly over the foot, and the feet should be placed with the toes pointing straight ahead. A pigeon-toed effect should be avoided. As the feet pass each other, the steps are small and close together, with the toes pointed straight ahead in the line of direction. The movement of the hips is merely the subtle result of the specific action of the feet and the knees. There should be no intentional swinging of the hip from side to side. There needs to be a stabilization of the upper trunk at the waist in order to keep it easily upright and the shoulders straight.

The head is held with the focus constantly on one's partner. The arm and hand, when free from partner, are held in a bent-elbow position, waist level, palm down. The man does not hold his partner close. There is seldom any body contact.

The Rumba, with its open and encircling patterns, is generally danced within a small space and reflects a dignified, although flirtatious, quality.

Teaching Suggestions for Rumba Style

First, practice the motion described above, moving forward in a slow, slow rhythm, working to achieve the feeling of the roll. Practice in front of a mirror is usually helpful. Second, practice the same motion forward in a slow quick quick rhythm (Cuban walk). Third, practice the motion as in the box step. Finally, practice with partner in closed dance position.

FUNDAMENTAL RUMBA STEPS

Directions are for the man, facing line of direction; woman's part is reversed, except as noted.

Basic Rumba Steps

CUBAN WALK

STEPS	4/4 COUNTS	RHYTHM CUE
Place L forward, roll weight slowly onto L	1–2	slow
Place R forward, roll weight quickly onto R	3	quick
Place L forward, roll weight quickly onto L	4	quick

STEP CUE: Place–roll roll roll.
1 - 2 3 4

STYLE: The roll is the springlike action of pressing into the floor. The knee of the free foot bends and leads the foot into its new position, followed by the transfer of weight to that foot.

NOTE: The Cuban walk step is used for all moving variations when not in closed position. It may move forward, backward, or in a circle.

■ BOX STEP

(Closed position)

STEPS	4/4 COUNTS	RHYTHM CUE
Place L forward, roll weight slowly onto L	1–2	slow
Place R sideward, roll weight quickly onto R	3	quick
Place L close to R, roll weight quickly to L	4	quick
Place R backward, roll weight slowly onto R	1–2	slow
Place L sideward, roll weight quickly onto L	3	quick
Place R close to L, roll weight quickly onto R	4	quick

Floor pattern

start

STEP CUE: Forward side close/back side close.

STYLE: The knee leads each step. The feet are placed flat on the floor, in a small box pattern.

LEAD: To lead a box step the man should use a forward body action followed by right-hand pressure and right elbow pull to the right to take the woman into the forward sequence of the box. Forward pressure of the right hand followed by pressure to the left side takes the woman into the back sequence of the box.

NOTE: Students need to understand that this forward, side, close constitutes the forward sequence or forward basic and that back, side, close constitutes the back sequence or back basic. These will be referred to in the variations.

■ *Rumba Step Variations*

- Box Turn
- Flirtation Break
- Side by Side
- Circular Turn
- Parallel Turn
- Bolero Break
  - Walk Around
  - Parallel Turn
  - Circular Turn
- Varsouvienne Break

■ BOX TURN

(Closed position)

The Rumba box step is the same foot pattern as the Westchester box step in the Foxtrot. The box turn will follow the same pattern as the Foxtrot box turn, p. 30. The style is different and one needs to shorten the step and add the Cuban movement.

Fundamental Rumba Steps (continued)

■ FLIRTATION BREAK

(Closed position)

Starting from closed position, dancers will change to flirtation position (see number 17, p. 9) and travel with the Cuban walk either forward or backward.

STEPS	4/4 COUNTS	RHYTHM CUE
Step L forward	1–2	slow
Step R sideward	3	quick
Close L to R, roll weight L	4	quick
Step R backward, a larger step changing to flirtation position, removing his right arm from around the woman	1–2	slow
Step L sideward	3	quick
Close R to L, roll weight to R	4	quick
Step L forward	1–2	slow
Step R forward	3	quick
Step L forward	4	quick
Step R forward	1–2	slow
Step L forward	3	quick
Step R forward	4	quick

STEP CUE: Slow quick quick.

STYLE: In flirtation position, the dances use the Cuban walk step, all forward or all back. The man steps back a little larger step when he is changing to flirtation position. Finger pressure and arm control are essential as they are the only way the man has to lead. The free arm is held up, elbow bent, parallel to the floor.

LEAD: To lead all turns, the man dips his shoulders in the direction of the turn and his upper torso turns before his leg and foot turn. The man's left-hand position changes to palm up, finger grasp in flirtation position. Man may lead with fingers to push the woman backward, or to pull to bring her forward. Pressure should come on the quick beats, so that change of direction actually occurs on the next slow.

NOTE: The man may lead as many steps in either direction as desired. To return to closed position and basic Rumba box step, the man will be moving the woman forward in flirtation position. During a back sequence on the right foot, the man will go into closed position as follows:

STEPS	4/4 COUNTS	RHYTHM CUE
Step R backward, pulling the woman into closed position	1–2	slow
Step L sideward, changing L-hand position	3	quick
Close R to L, roll to R	4	quick
Step L forward into the forward sequence		

■ SIDE BY SIDE

(Flirtation position)

Starting from flirtation position with the couple traveling either forward or backward in flirtation position, the man turns one-quarter to the right (woman to the left), to side-by-side position, woman on the man's left.

LEAD: On the quick quick beats, his left hand guides her into side-by-side position. She must then press with her arm against the man's arm or wrist to follow the leads in this position. The man may direct them forward or backward in this position, changing on the quick beats.

▪ CIRCULAR TURN

(Side-by-side position)

Starting from side-by-side position, the couple is traveling forward. The man on the quick beats will change his direction so as to move backward, pulling with his lead hand toward himself to direct the woman to continue forward. This will result in a turn clockwise, side by side. They should focus on each other over the shoulder.

a. Side-by-side position

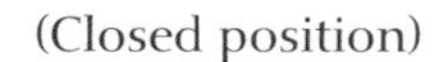

b. Circular turn (man moves backward)

NOTE: The man may return to basic box when he is on a back sequence with the right foot by facing the woman, taking close position, guiding into the quick quick beats sideward left, and starting the forward sequence on the left foot.

▪ PARALLEL TURN

(Starting from circular turn)

When traveling in circular turn, the man backward, the woman forward, the man on the quick beats will turn suddenly one-half counterclockwise into right parallel position and, turning clockwise, both man and woman will be moving forward, around each other. Return to basic box as noted above.

a. Circular turn: man moving backward, woman forward

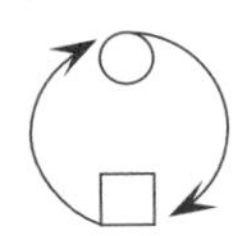

b. Parallel turn: both man and woman move forward

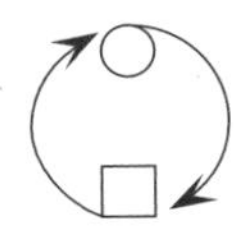

▪ BOLERO BREAK

(Closed position)

Starting in closed dance position, the dancers execute the forward sequence of the box step. Then, as the man starts the back sequence, he turns the woman clockwise under his left arm. The man continues to take the box step in place while the woman travels in a circular pattern clockwise until she faces him again at arm's distance. He has maintained hand contact (his left, her right) during this time and he finally guides her forward toward him back into closed dance position.

STEP CUE: Slow quick quick.

STYLE: The woman will use the Cuban walk when moving around clockwise and keep the man's rhythm until back in closed position. She should keep the body upright, outside arm up and focus on her partner.

LEAD: The man gives the lead by lifting his left hand high enough so that the woman does not have to duck her head to get under his arm. He also guides her under with his right hand. His left hand guides her around clockwise and finally draws her toward him to closed position.

NOTE: Any number of basic sequences (slow quick quick) may be taken, and, if the partners both keep the pattern going, they can move right back into the box step when they come together in closed position.

Fundamental Rumba Steps (continued)

▪ VARIATIONS OF BOLERO BREAK

1. *Walk Around.* As the woman comes around from Bolero break, instead of going into closed position, the man with his left hand will lead the woman toward his right side and past his right shoulder, bringing her around behind him and toward his left side. He then turns one-half left to face her, and they move into closed dance position.

STEP CUE: Slow quick quick.

STYLE: The woman will use Cuban walk and keep her circle in close to the man. The man will keep the box step going until she passes his right side, and then he will go into the Cuban walk on a forward sequence and come around to his left to meet her. Both focus on each other. From closed position:

a. Bolero break

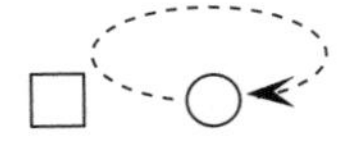

b. Walk around

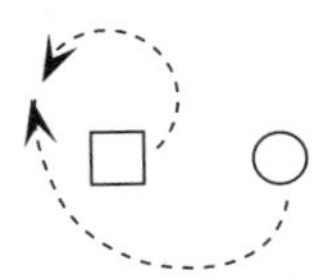

LEAD: The man should raise his left arm high enough so that he does not have to duck his head as she goes around. He will move under his own left arm and turn left to meet the woman.

NOTE: When the man and woman meet, they should go back into closed position and box step on whichever foot is free.

2. *Parallel Turn.* As the woman comes around in her wide arc at arm's distance, the man will move in toward her, coming into right parallel position, and they will turn clockwise as far as desired. The man may then lead woman to closed position or twirl the woman clockwise once around in place to finish in closed position. The lead for the twirl should come as the man steps into the forward basic sequence with the left foot so that the woman may turn on one basic step starting with her right foot. They finish together in the back part of the box step in closed position.

STEP CUE: Slow quick quick.

STYLE: They use the Cuban walk. Focus on each other.

a. Bolero break

b. Man moves forward to parallel position

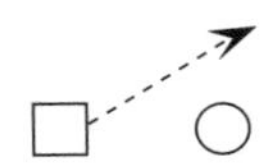

c. Parallel turn

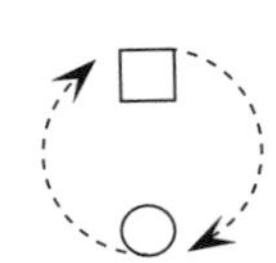

3. *Circular Turn.* Immediately after the man turns the woman under his left arm to start the Bolero break, he brings his left arm down to a pressure position against her right elbow and turns one-quarter right to be in a side-by-side position. Then the man moves backward, the woman forward, turning in place clockwise. To get out of this turn, the man turns to face the woman and steps back with his right foot into the back basic sequence, taking closed dance position.

STEP CUE: Slow quick quick.

STYLE: They must be in a tight side-by-side position. They will use the Cuban walk. Focus should be on the partner, outside arm up.

LEAD: Firmness in the arm is necessary by man and response to this firm pressure is needed by the woman.

▪ VARSOUVIENNE BREAK

(Closed position)

This is a delightful series of turns with the couple rolling from one to the other all the while keeping the basic Cuban walk rhythm, slow quick quick, going in the feet. There are four changes of position that should be practiced before the rhythm is added.

1. *Turn into the Varsouvienne Position:* The man releases the woman's right hand and reaches across in front of his right shoulder to take her left hand, pulling it across in front of him, causing the woman to turn clockwise a half-turn until she is by his right side, facing in the same direction. The man now holds the woman's left hand in his left and has his right around her waist to take her right hand at her right side. They circle clockwise one complete turn. To do this effectively, the man moves forward, the woman backward to turn in place.
2. *Turn into Reverse Varsouvienne Position:* The man releases the woman's right hand and turns to his own right, bringing their joined left hands across in front of woman as she turns left until she is by his left side and slightly behind him, facing in the same direction. She reaches around behind him with her right hand to take his right hand at his right side. They continue to circle clockwise another complete turn, the man now moving backward, the woman forward.
3. *Return to Varsouvienne Position:* The man releases the woman's right hand and, turning to his left, brings their joined left hands across in front of him, turning the woman halfway around clockwise until she is to the right of the man. His right arm is around her waist, holding her right hand. They continue turning clockwise, the man again moving forward, the woman backward, one full time around.
4. *Turn Back to Closed Position:* The man releases the woman's left hand and by pulling with his right toward him he turns the woman clockwise halfway around into closed dance position. He changes her right hand into his left and the man leads into the basic box step, usually on the back sequence with his right foot.

STEP CUE: Slow quick quick or change quick quick.

STYLE: Although this is described in four parts, the transitions into each part should be smooth so as to make the entire maneuver blend into one figure rather than four disconnected parts. There is no set number of Cuban walk steps to be taken for each part. The couple should turn continuously clockwise throughout the figure. Dancers should be careful to maintain good Rumba style throughout.

RUMBA COMBOS

The Rumba routines are combinations for practice, listed from simple to complex. (Closed position, unless otherwise indicated.)

1. *Cuban Walk and Box*
   4 Cuban walks
   2 box steps
2. *Box and Bolero Break*
   2 box steps
   Bolero break
3. *Box and Flirtation Step*
   2 box steps
   flirtation break forward and back
4. *Bolero Break and Walk Around*
   2 box steps
   Bolero break and walk around
5. *Bolero Break and Parallel Turn*
   2 box steps
   Bolero break
   parallel turn
6. *Flirtation Break and Reverse Turn*
   2 box steps
   flirtation break
   side by side
   parallel turn

Salsa

Cut-time

	Q	Q	S
¢	1	&	2

SALSA MUSIC ENTERED THE dance scene in the mid-1960s when the Cubans settled in Miami and southern Florida. Their Latin music became a blend of Afro-Cuban jazz. *Salsa* is the Spanish word for *sauce* and, as the Spanish sauces are spicy, the name seems appropriate.

The Salsa is written in 4/4 cut time. The rhythm is quick, quick, slow. It is counted 1 and 2 of the cut-time beat. The music is fast and lighthearted.

SALSA STYLE

Salsa Steps

The style is very similar to the rumba: bent knees, *small flat footsteps* (weight over the heel), hip action of the Cuban walk as it rolls, and upper body held firmly poised, never sagging, rib cage moving subtly side to side, following the action of the feet.

Directions are for the man, woman's part reversed, except as noted.

BASIC STEP

(Closed position)

STEPS	C COUNTS	RHYTHM CUE
Step L forward	1	quick
Step R backward	*and*	quick
Step L beside R	2	slow
Step R backward	1	quick
Step L forward	*and*	quick
Step R beside L	2	slow

Use basic step to turn L or R in place.

SIDE STEP

(Closed position)

Step sideways L	1	quick
Close R to L	*and*	quick
Step sideways L	2	slow
Reverse to R	1 *and* 2	quick, quick, slow

▪ CROSS STEP

(Two hands joined)

Cross L over R (with exaggeration)	1	quick
Step back R	*and*	quick
Step L close to R	2	slow

Repeat crossing R.

▪ THROW OUT

(Closed position)

2 Basic Steps (LRL, RLR).

Man releases his right hand, gives the woman a slight push, and takes 2 more Basic Steps in place.

The woman moves away from partner (R, L, R) and comes back (L, R, L) to closed position.

Samba

THE *SAMBA*, FROM BRAZIL, is the most active of the Latin American dances. It was introduced to the United States about 1929. It is interesting to discover how similar it is to some of the native dance rhythms of Africa. The Samba is sensitive and smooth. The music is fiery, yet lyrical; and the dance is characterized by tiny, light footwork, and the rise and fall of the body (always turning and at the same time swaying back and forth at a most deceiving pendular angle).

SAMBA RHYTHM

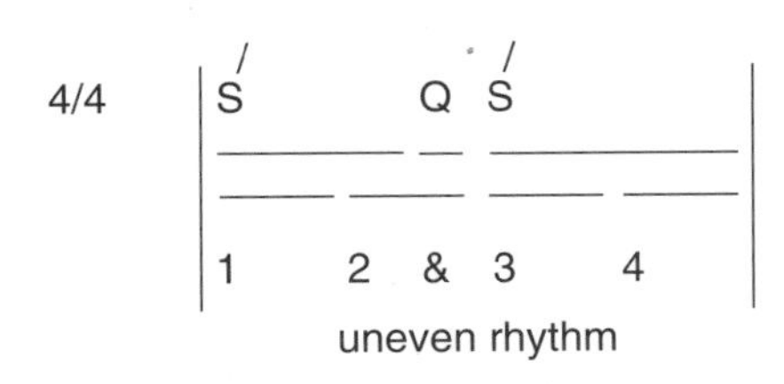

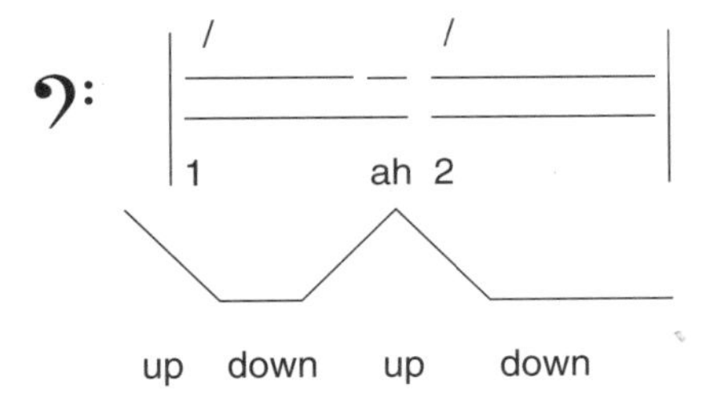

Samba is written in 4/4 cut time and may be either slow or fast, although it is generally preferred at the faster tempo. The rhythm is slow quick slow, an uneven rhythm pattern. It has a double accent, one on each of the two major beats, and these downbeats are represented by the down movements of the dance. It will be counted as 1 *ah* 2 of the cut-time beat.

The execution of the up down weight change is the secret to the smooth, springing rhythm. There is a change of weight from one foot to the other on each of the three beats, down up down, but a preliminary uplift of the body on the upbeat of the music sets the rhythmical swing in motion. The music is fast and lighthearted.

Samba (continued)

SAMBA STYLE

In contrast to the Rumba, which has a lower body movement, the Samba has a total body action. The easy springing motion comes from the ball of the foot, the flexible ankle, and the easy relaxed knees. The upper body is held firmly poised, never sagging, and it seems to sway forward and back about an axis that centers in the pelvic area. The arm, when not in contact with partner, is held out from the body, a little above waist level, bent at the elbow, parallel to the floor, palm down. The first accented step, count 1, is the largest of the three steps, the other two being like a quick-change weight step. It has been called a "step-ball-change" in the language of tap dancing. It is important to get the correct rhythm and foot pattern before working on the body sway. However, having that mastered, the body sways backward as the feet take the forward basic and forward as the feet take the back basic. Always the pattern is small and on the ball of the foot.

FUNDAMENTAL SAMBA STEPS

Directions are for man; woman's part reversed, except as noted.

▪ BASIC STEP

(Forward and back; Closed position)

STEPS	4/4 COUNTS	RHYTHM CUE
Step L forward	1	slow
Step R forward next to L	*ah*	quick
Step L in place	2	slow
Step R backward	1	slow
Step L backward beside R	*ah*	quick
Step R in place	2	slow

STEP CUE: Forward change weight/back change weight.

STYLE: The steps are small. Feet are close together on the change step. The rise and fall of the body begins on the upbeat with the rise of the body. This is the preparatory motion for each step. With the first step, the down motion is executed on the first slow beat, followed by an up motion on the quick beat and down again on the slow beat. The body is controlled. It does not bend at the waist.

LEAD: With the increased pressure of his right hand, the man sways backward slightly when stepping forward with his left foot and sways forward when stepping backward with his right foot. The woman sways forward when the man sways backward, backward when he sways forward, so that the appearance is a rocking action parallel to each other.

▪ *Samba Step Variations*

Basic Turn	Slow Side Close	Copa Step
Forward Progressive Step	Sideward Basic	

▪ BASIC TURN

(Closed position, counterclockwise)

STEPS	4/4 COUNTS	RHYTHM CUE
Step L forward, turning one-quarter counterclockwise	1	slow
Step R forward beside L	*ah*	quick
Step L beside R	2	slow

Step R backward, toe in, and turn one-quarter counterclockwise	1	slow
Step L backward beside R	*ah*	quick
Step R beside L	2	slow

STEP CUE: Turn step step.

STYLE: Keep the down up down motion going. Sway backward and then forward.

LEAD: Bank right arm in direction of turn, and pull into the back step.

NOTE: It is important to turn on a small base, turning on the ball of the foot, not trying to step sideward around partner.

■ FORWARD PROGRESSIVE STEP

(Closed position)

STEPS	¢ COUNTS	RHYTHM CUE
Step L forward	1	slow
Step R beside L	*ah*	quick
Step L beside R	2	slow
Step R backward, changing from closed position to two hands joined with partner	1	slow
Step L beside R	*ah*	quick
Step R beside L, drop L hand	2	slow
Into Forward Progressive Step (Side-by-side position)		
Step L forward and diagonally outward to the L (woman R)	1	slow
Step R beside L	*ah*	quick
Step L beside R	2	slow
Step R forward and diagonally inward toward partner (woman L)	1	slow
Step L beside R	*ah*	quick
Step R beside L	2	slow
Back to Closed Position		
Step L, turning diagonally outward	1	slow
Step R beside L	*ah*	quick
Step L beside R	2	slow
Step R, turning diagonally inward, and take closed position	1	slow
Step L beside R	*ah*	quick
Step R beside L	2	slow
Into basic, step forward on the left foot		

STEP CUE: Forward step step change step step/out step step in step step/out step step close step step/forward step step back step step.

STYLE: The couple turns only diagonally away from each other and back, not back to back. When they come in, the outside hand, which is up turning with the body, touches partner's hand, palm to palm. Arm when free stays up.

LEAD: The man's right hand controls the motion and the diagonal position by reaching forward and back with the hand as he turns.

NOTE: The diagonal step should reach in the line of direction each time, so that the couple will progress down the floor. The progressive step may be repeated over and over as desired.

Fundamental Samba Steps (continued)

▪ SLOW SIDE CLOSE

(Closed position)

A resting step.

STEPS	¢ COUNTS	RHYTHM CUE
Step L sideward	1	slow
Close R to L, take weight R	2	slow

Repeat three times moving left. The last time, do not take weight right but be ready to go back the other direction. Take four side-close steps to the right.

STEP CUE: Side close side close.

STYLE: The sway of the Samba is discontinued as is the down up down motion. The rhythm is an even-beat step close.

LEAD: Following a basic Samba step forward and back, the man has his left foot free. Stopping the sway and motion by control of his body and right arm, he steps left sideward into the pattern. Check lead indication 4, p. 10.

NOTE: Many beginners find the Samba basic step very tiring, so this step may be used to permit the dancers a resting variation.

▪ SIDEWARD BASIC

(Closed position)

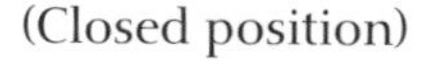

STEPS	¢ COUNTS	RHYTHM CUE
Step L sideward	1	slow
Step R behind L heel	*ah*	quick
Step L in place	2	slow
Step R sideward	1	slow
Step L behind R heel	*ah*	quick
Step R in place	2	slow

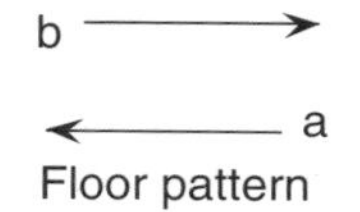

Floor pattern

STEP CUE: Side back step/side back step.

STYLE: Both man and woman may rock the body and turn the head in the direction away from the leading foot. The steps are small. A long step is awkward.

LEAD: The man directs the sideward step with his right arm, but the body leans in the opposite direction.

NOTE: For variation, the man may (1) turn the woman one-quarter counterclockwise as he steps to the left side, so that she turns her back on the direction they are traveling. As he repeats the step to the right, he turns her a half-turn clockwise. (2) They may both turn from reverse open position to open position.

▪ COPA STEP

(Open position)

STEPS	¢ COUNTS	RHYTHM CUE
Step L forward	1	slow
Step R back in place on ball of foot, leaving the L foot forward	*ah*	quick
Drag L foot back half the distance, taking weight on L	2	slow
Step R forward	1	slow
Step L back in place on ball of foot, leaving R foot forward	*ah*	quick
Drag R foot back half the distance, taking weight R	2	slow

STEP CUE: Down up drag.

STYLE: The left step forward is flat with the knee bending, and the body leans backward slightly. The right step backward on the ball of the foot is accompanied by a raise of the body, which stays up during the drag of the left foot backward.

LEAD: The man leads into the open position on the back right sequence of the basic step and then starts the copa with the left foot in open position. The man leads the copa action by a back lean and down up up action in the body.

NOTE: Dragging the foot only halfway back allows the copa step, when repeated over and over, to progress forward in open position. If the man opens in reverse open position, the copa will begin on the inside foot.

SAMBA COMBOS

The Samba routines are combinations for practice, listed from simple to complex. (Closed position, unless otherwise indicated.)

1. *Basic Slow Side Close*
   8 basic (forward and backward)
   8 side close (4 left, 4 right)
2. *Basic Step and Turn*
   4 basic steps
   4 turning left
   8 side close (4 left, 4 right)
3. *Basic: Forward and Sideward*
   8 basic (forward and backward)
   4 sideward steps
4. *Basic Turn—Copa*
   4 basic turn
   4 slow side close
   4 copa steps
5. *Advanced Combo*
   4 basic
   4 sideward basic
   8 forward progressive
   8 copa steps (open)
6. *Advanced Combo*
   4 basic
   8 copa steps
   8 basic turn
   4 slow side close

6 Mixers and Ice Breakers

MIXERS AND ICE BREAKERS

The social purposes of any dance group, be it a class or party, are greatly enriched by the use of "mixers and breakers." Ice breakers are simple line and circle dances that do not involve a partner. They are particularly useful as pre-class pre-party warm-ups for early arrivals. Mixers provide participants an opportunity to socialize within a group. Mixers are generally designed to involve all participants en masse or in an accumulative fashion. Opening activities of this nature help establish a fun and informal atmosphere, assure quick and easy accomplishment, and add variety to the occasion.

Gain or Exchange Partners

1. **Upset the Cherry Basket:** When the music stops, the leader requests that everyone change partners. If couples are asked to change with the couple nearest them, everyone is involved, and no one walks to the side for the lack of a partner.
2. **Snowball, Whistle Dance, Pony Express, or Multiplication Dance:** One to three couples start to dance. When the music stops, each couple separates and goes to the sidelines and gets a new partner. This is repeated until everyone is dancing.
3. **Line Up:** The men line up on one side of the room, facing the wall; the women on the other side, facing the wall. When the signal is given, each line backs up until they gain a new partner.
4. **Arches:** All the dancers form a single circle and walk counterclockwise around the circle. Two couples form arches on opposite sides of the circle. When the music stops, the arch is lowered. Those caught in the arch go to the center of the circle, gain a partner, and go back to the circle to form new arches. Eventually, just a few dancers will be walking through the tunnel of arches. When all have partners, the dancing proceeds.

5. **Star by the Right:** Six men form a right-hand star in the center of a single circle formed by the group. The star moves clockwise, and the circle counterclockwise. As the leader gives the signal, six women hook onto the star; alternate sexes are called out until all have hooked onto the star. A little spice is added if the last person on each spoke winks or beckons a specific person from the ring to join his or her spoke. When the star is completed the woman dances with the man on her right.
6. **Matching:** Advertising slogans (Ivory Soap–99.9 percent pure, it floats), split proverbs (a rolling stone–gathers no moss), famous couples (Romeo–Juliet), pairs of words that belong together (ham–eggs), playing cards (spades match with hearts for each number, clubs with diamonds), pictures cut in half (cartoons), or songs may be used for this mixer. Half of the slips of paper are given to the men, and the corresponding halves are distributed to the women. As the people circulate, they try to find the person with the corresponding half of their slogan, proverb, cartoon, or whatever has been selected to be matched. When everyone has found his or her partner, the dancing proceeds. If songs are used, each person sings his or her song until he or she finds the person singing the same song.
7. **Musical Chairs:** Set up a double row of chairs, back to back, almost the length of the room. Leave space between every group of four chairs so that partners can get together. The group marches around the chairs. When the music stops, each person tries to gain a seat. A man must sit back to back with a woman. These two become partners and proceed to dance while all the others continue to play the game until all have partners. When all are dancing, the next signal is given and partners separate and rush for a chair, thus providing a change of partners. **Musical knees:** Played like musical chairs, except that on a signal, the men get down on one knee and the women rush to sit on a knee. Those left out go to the side.
8. **Ice Cube Pass:** Double circle men on the outside, women on inside. Pass an orange around men's circle; an ice cube around the women's circle. When the music stops, the man with the orange and woman with the ice cube step to center of circle or its outside and become partners. Repeat over and over, until all have partners. Several oranges and ice cubes may be passed simultaneously.
9. **Mexican Broom Dance:*** As couples are dancing, an extra man with a broom knocks the broom handle on the floor several times. Partners separate, women line up on left side of man with the broom and men on right side. The two lines are about five feet part. All clap their hands while lining up and until they get a new partner. After everyone is in line, the man with the broom goes up and down the line and decides with which woman he wants to dance. When he has made his choice, he drops the broom and grabs his partner, while everyone else takes a partner too, and dancing resumes. Then the extra man picks up the broom and the procedure starts all over again. More fun is added to the mixer if the man, in going up and down the line, pretends to drop the broom but actually keeps on looking for a better partner.

*Herb Greggerson, author of *Herb's Blue Bonnet Calls,* saw this mixer danced in Mexico and presented it for the first time at a Square Dance institute at the University of Texas, April 1948. Directions were first printed in *Foot 'n' Fiddle,* Editors, Anne Pittman, Marlys Swenson, and Olcutt Sanders, may 1948, p. 4.

■ *Trade Dances*

1. **Are You on the Beam?** While everyone is dancing, a spotlight is suddenly focused on a specific area. Those people standing in the rays of the light are requested to give a yell, sing a song, or trade partners.
2. **Hats Off!** Four hats are distributed among four couples. Each couple with a hat places it on one member of another couple. When the music stops, the couples with the hats must change partners.

■ *Tags*

1. **Women's Tag or Men's Tag:** Certain dances may be designed as women's tag or men's tag.
2. **Similarity Tag:** Either a man or a woman may tag, but the person tagging can only tag someone who has a similar color of hair, eyes, shirt, shoes, and so on.
3. **"You Take the Lemon, I'll Take the Peach":** A few lemons or other designated articles are distributed among the men or the women. Anyone who holds the article may tag. Additional fun may be had by stopping the music periodically and anyone holding the article pays a forfeit. Later the forfeits are redeemed by performing a humorous stunt.

■ *Elimination Dances*

1. **Number Please?** Each couple is given a number. Each time the music stops, a number is called out and the couple or couples having the numbers called sit down. Numbers are called out until only one couple remains.
2. **Lemon Dance:** An object–for example, a lemon–is passed from couple to couple. When the music stops, the couple with the object sits down. Eventually one couple is left.
3. **Dance Contest:** Determine the type of dancing for the contest, for example, Waltz or Jitterbug. It should be conducted in a casual manner with qualified judges. Gradually, the contestants are eliminated until one or two couples remain. Choosing two couples, instead of one, for the winners keeps competition from becoming too keen.
4. **Orange Dance:** Each couple balances an orange or a tennis ball between their foreheads and proceeds to dance. Slow music like a Tango allows the dancers to concentrate on keeping the orange in position and still move to the music. When a couple drops the orange, they go to the sidelines. Eventually one couple is left and the rest have enjoyed the antics of those trying to keep the orange in position. Change the rhythm of the music to match the ability of the dancers.

LINE AND CIRCLE MIXERS

Pre-class or pre-party dance activities that are set to popular music or spirited march tunes. These activities generally accommodate any number of single dancers in an accumulative fashion thus generating a festive atmosphere to begin an occasion.

Bunny Hop

METER: 4/4. Directions are presented in beats.

MUSIC: Any schottische or music specific for Bunny Hop.

FORMATION: Single line (conga line), hands placed on waist or shoulders of dancer ahead.

DIRECTIONS FOR THE DANCE

■ *Beats*

Starting position: feet together, weight on both feet.

1–4 Hop right, touch left heel out to the side (beats 1–2), Hop right, touch left toe near right foot (beats 3–4). Repeat. (Action is quick, quick, quick quick).

5–8 Beginning with hop on left, repeat action of beats 1–4.

9–10 Jump forward (slow). Weight on both feet.

11–12 Jump backward (slow). Weight on both feet.

13–16 Take three jumps forward (quick, quick, quick, hold).

NOTE: Leader leads line in any direction around the room. Avoid cutting through other lines!

Conga

METER: 4/4. Directions presented in beats.

MUSIC: Any conga (Latin type) music.

FORMATION: Single file line, hands placed on waist of dancer ahead.

DIRECTIONS FOR THE DANCE

Beats

Starting position: feet together, weight on both.

1 Beginning left, step forward.
2 Step right forward.
3 Step left forward.
4 Kick right foot to side (right knee turns in).
5 Step right forward.
6 Step left forward.
7 Step right forward.
8 Kick left foot to side (left knee turns in).

NOTE: Leader leads line in any direction around the room. Do not travel through other lines.

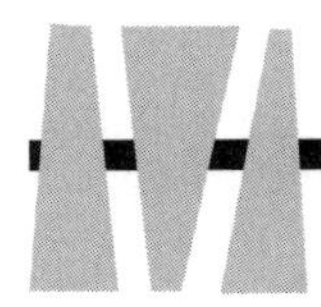

Grand March

LET THE DANCE BEGIN! *Grand March* has long been a part of American dance tradition. At ceremonial occasions and balls, the instrumental groups would play a short concert prior to the dancing. Then the floor managers of the ball would signal for the dance to begin. The instrumentalists would play a march and the couples would begin a grand promenade around the room for the Grand March. Today, for special

Grand March (continued)

occasions, dance festivals, and one-night stand dance parties, the Grand March is part of the program. It may not be first but perhaps after the intermission. Dancers look forward to that moment of everyone dancing together; winding in and out from one pattern to the next.

The Grand March may be used as an end in itself, since it is impressive and stimulates group feeling, or it may be used as a means for organizing a group quickly for another activity. A Grand March is most effective when many people participate. Therefore when scheduling a Grand March, consider that guests do not always arrive punctually.

MUSIC: Any lively March, Two-Step, or Square Dance tune.

POSITION: Escort.

FORMATION: Double circle, couples facing the line of direction, or single files, men in one and women in the other.

DIRECTIONS FOR THE GRAND MARCH

Leadership

The leader stands at either the front or the rear of the room. A change in pattern is indicated as the group nears the leader. It is helpful if the first two or three couples are familiar with the various figures to be used in the Grand March. Experienced couples will follow the leader's cues more easily and set the pattern for the others to follow. An assistant standing at the end opposite the leader facilitates the flow.

Beginning

A Grand March may be started either from two single files of individuals (particularly suited for groups not already acquainted) or in couples.

1. **Two single files:** Men line up on one side of the room and women on the other. Both files face either the front or the rear of the room as indicated by the leader. Note: The leader must be careful to indicate the proper direction for the two files to face so that the women will be on the right side of the men when couples are formed. Each line marches toward the end of the room, turns, and marches toward the opposite line. The files meet, forming couples in escort position, the women to the right of the men, and march down the center of the room.
2. **Couples in a double circle:** Couples in escort position form a double circle and march counterclockwise. One couple is selected as the leader and that couple, followed by the others, moves down the center of the room.

Figures

These figures may be used in any order as long as they flow from one to the other.

1. **Single files**
   A. **Inner and outer circle.** When each couple reaches the front of the room, partners separate, men left and women right, and travel down the side of the room until they meet at the opposite end. Then the lines pass each other. The women travel on the inside, men on the outside, and down the side of the room until they meet again at the front of the room. They pass again, the

men traveling on the inside, women on the outside, and down the sides of the room.

B. **The Cross (X).** When each file reaches the rear corner, the leader of each file makes an abrupt turn and travels diagonally toward the front corner on the opposite side. Both files cross in the center of the room, the woman crossing in front of her partner. The files travel down the side of the room toward the rear corners. The diagonal cross is repeated, the man crossing in front of his partner.

C. **Virginia Reel.** Couples move down the center in double file. When each couple reaches the front of the room, partners separate, men left, women right, and travel down the sides of the room to form two files about 10 to 15 feet apart. Both lines face each other. The head woman and the foot man meet in the middle and dance away. Then the head man and the foot woman meet in the middle in like manner and dance away. This process is repeated until all have partners and are dancing.

2. **Couples**

A. **Four, eight, or sixteen abreast.** When the couples marching down the center arrive at the front of the room, the lead couple turns to the right, marches to the side of the room, and back toward the rear of the room. The second couple turns left, the third right, and so on, and march to the side and back to the rear of the room. When they meet at the rear of the room, the two approaching couples march down the center of the room together, thus forming a group of four abreast. At the front of the room each group of four marches alternately to the right and left, down the sides, and at the rear of the room they form a line eight abreast. The same procedure is followed to form lines of 16 or more abreast. After the group has formed lines of 16 abreast they may be instructed to mark time in place.

B. **"Ring up" for squares.** If groups of eight are desired for the next activity, for example, a Square Dance, the couples mark time when they are eight abreast. Each line of eight then "rings up," or makes a circle.

C. **Over and under.** When the couples are four abreast, the two couples separate at the front of the room, one turning right, the other left. When the couples meet at the rear of the room, the first couple of the double file on the right side of the room makes an arch. The first couple of the other double file goes under the arch and quickly makes an arch for the second couple they meet. All couples in both double files are alternately making an arch or traveling under an arch.

D. **Snake out.** Then the couples are 8 or 16 abreast, the person on the right end of the front line leads that line in single file to the right of the column of dancers and in between lines two and three. As the person on the left end of the first line passes the person on the right end of the second line, they join hands and line two then follows line one. The leader then leads the line between lines three and four and again as the last person in the moving line passes the right end of the third line, they join hands and line three joins with lines one and two. The moving line weaves in and out of the remaining lines and each time the person on the end of the moving line passes the right end of the next line they join hands and continue weaving in and out. After all lines have been "snaked out," the leader may lead the line in serpentine fashion around the room and eventually circle the room clockwise in a single circle, all facing the center.

E. **Danish march.** When the couples are in a double circle or double file, partners face and stand about 4 feet apart. The first couple joins hands holding arms out at shoulder height and slides the length of the formation used. The second couple follows, and so on. When couples reach the end, they join the group. This may be repeated with partners standing back-to-back as they slide.

Grand March (continued)

F. **Grand right and left.** When couples are in a single circle, partners face and start a grand right and left. This may continue until partners meet or until the leader signals for new partners to be taken for a promenade or other figure.

G. **Paul Jones.** When couples are in a single circle, any of the figures for a Paul Jones may be used. See page 000.

Ending

There is no set ending for a Grand March. However, the ending should be definite so there is a feeling of completion and satisfaction. It may end with people in groups for the next activity or in a circle with everyone joining in a song or with dancers swinging into a Waltz, a Polka, or some other planned activity.

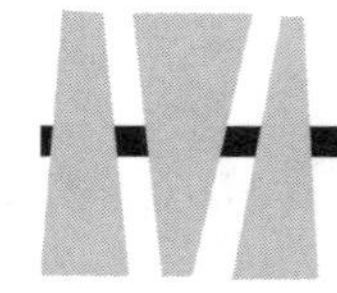

Hokey Pokey

HOKEY POKEY IS A MODERN Play Part Game popular with young and old, an adaptation of Lobby Lou. The music was written in 1947 by the Sun Valley Trio, Tafft Baker, Larry La Prise, and Charles Macak, natives of Washington. Tafft Baker wrote the words and tried them out on his girlfriend Jean. Jean and Tafft married and traveled around the United States promoting the song and dance. Acuff-Rose Opryland Music pressed the record in 1950 and the rest is history. The action sequence on several records with calls varies slightly from the one given here. The tune is simple and may easily be done without musical accompaniment. The leader may sing the call for the group or have the group sing and perform the action.

RECORDS: Can-Ed DC 74528, LS E38; Capitol 6026, EZ726; MacGregor 6995.

CASSETTE: DC 13X.

FORMATION: Single circle, individuals face center; or single circle, couples face center, woman to right of partner.

DIRECTIONS FOR THE DANCE

Call

You put your right foot in. Place foot forward into circle.

You put your right foot out. Place foot back away from circle.

You put your right foot in.

And you shake it all about. Shake foot toward center of circle.

You do the hokey pokey. Place palms together above head and Rumba hips.

And you turn yourself around. Individuals shake arms above head and turn around. If couples, man turns woman on left once and a half with right elbow and progresses one position clockwise.

That's what it's all about. Clap hands four times.

Repeat the above call, substituting the following parts of the body: left foot, right arm, left arm, right elbow, head, right hip, whole self, backside.

Ending

You do the hokey pokey.
You do the hokey pokey. Raise the arms above head and lower arms and head in a bowing motion.
You do the hokey pokey. Kneel on both knees and raise arms above head and lower arms and head in a bowing motion.
That's what it's all about. Slap the floor six times.

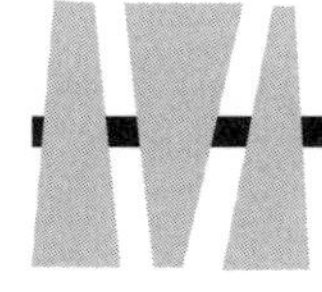

Paul Jones Your Lady

DURING THE NINETEENTH CENTURY, the group dances with set figures, like the Quadrille, the Lancers, and the *Paul Jones,* allowed for the interchange of partners. Paul Jones, formerly danced in the ballroom and frequently used as the first dance at a party, is still danced today as a lively mixer. In some parts of the West, the same dance is called *Circle Two-Step* or *Brownee.*

MUSIC: Any lively two-step.

POSITION: Promenade.

FORMATION: Double circle, couples facing line of direction.

STEPS: Shuffle, Two-Step.

DIRECTIONS FOR THE MIXER

The leader calls out each figure and signals clearly. Each figure is danced briefly as it is merely a method of changing partners.

I. PAUL JONES YOUR LADY OR PROMENADE

Couples promenade around room in one large circle.

II. FIGURES

A. **Single circle.** Couples form a single circle, hands joined. Slide left, right, and/or shuffle to center and back. Each man takes his corner woman for a new partner.

B. **The basket.** Women form an inner circle, hands joined, and slide left. Men form an outer circle, hands joined, and slide right. Both circles stop. Men raise joined hands. Women move backward through arches made by men and stand beside a man. Men lower arms. Everyone slides left, then right. Each man takes the woman on right for a new partner.

Paul Jones Your Lady (continued)

C. **Across the circle.** Couples form a single circle, hands joined. Slide left, right, and shuffle to center, back, and center. Each man takes the woman across the circle as a new partner.

D. **Grand right and left.** Couples form a single circle, hands joined. Slide left, right, and shuffle to center and back. Face partner and grand right and left around the circle. Each man takes the woman facing him or the woman whose hand he holds when leader signals for new partners.

E. **Gentlemen kneel.** Couples form single circle and face partners. Men kneel, women move in reverse line of direction, weaving in and out between kneeling men. Each man takes the woman facing him when leader signals for new partners.

F. **Count off.** Double circle, couples facing counterclockwise. Women stand still and men move forward, counting off as many women as indicated by leader. Men may stand still while women move forward and count off in like manner.

▪ III. TWO-STEP

Couples in closed position, Two-Step about the room. Upon signal "Paul Jones Your Lady," they again fall into a double circle and promenade counterclockwise around room until the signal for a new figure action is given.

APPENDIX A:

Periodicals

Amateur Dancers The official membership publication of the United States Ballroom Dancers Association, Inc. Editorial Offices: Robert Meyer, Editor East, 1427 Gibsonwood Rd, Baltimore, MD 21228, Phone and Fax: (410) 747-7855. Joan Adams, Editor West, 16755 Wallingford Avenue North, Seattle, WA 98133. Phone and Fax: (206) 542-1639.

Ballroom Dancing Times Clerkenwell House, 45–47 Clerkenwell Green, London, England: EC1R OEB.

Country Dance Lines Magazine Drawer 139, Woodacre, CA 94973, (415) 488-0154.

Dancing USA 10600 University Avenue NW, Minneapolis, MN 55448-6166. (612) 757-4414, Fax: (612) 757-6605.

APPENDIX B:

Organizations and Resources

Ballroom Dance Camps, Conferences, and Workshops 155 Harman Building, Brigham Young University, Provo, Utah 84602. (801) 378-4851.

College Ballroom Dance Association Newsletter editor: Suzanne Zelink-Geldys, HPERD 116 Warner Hall, Eastern Michigan University, Ypsilanti, MI 48197. (313) 487-4388.

National Teachers Association of Country & Western Dance Ms. Kelly Gillette, President, 1817 Lamp Lighter Lane, Las Vegas, NV 89104.

The United States Amateur Ballroom Dancers Association, Inc. Editor East: Robert Meyer, 1427 Gibsonwood Rd., Baltimore, MD 21228. Phone and Fax: (410) 747-7855.
Editor West: Joan Adams, 16755 Wallingford Avenue North, Seattle, WA 98133. Phone and Fax: (206) 542-1639.

Music and Instructional Aids

Music for Social Dance or Ballroom Dance is subject to the particular "sound" in vogue at a particular point-in-time. "Standards" are tunes that are recognized by musicians and the public alike as favorite and do, indeed, survive several generations. At present, music for dancing is available in the form of CDs, Cassettes and videos. Sources listed under "General" carry some if not all types of music listed.

GENERAL

A Muse-A-Mood Co, 128 Hancock Place NE, Leesburg, VA 22075. Audio-Visual Catalogue, books, manuals, instructional tapes and videos. Booklets covering dance steps (beginners to advanced), history of swing, and music fundamentals.

Floyd's Record Shop, P.O. Box 10, 434 E. Main St., Ville Platte, Louisiana 70586; (318) 363-4893 or 1 (800) 738-8668. Features Cajun music.

Dance Vision USA, 4270 Cameron Street, Ste. 3A, Las Vegas, NV 89103. Catalogue of instructional videos, tapes, and CDs. Phone: 1 (800) 851-2813, Fax: 1 (702) 365-6644.

Louisiana Catalog, 148939 West Main St., Cut Off, Louisiana 70345-9436; (318) 632-4100 or 1 (800) 375-4100, Fax (504) 632-4129. Cajun music source.

Living Traditions, 2442 NW Market St, #168, Seattle, WA 98107, (206) 781-1238 or 1 (800) 500-2364. Source for videos, CDs and Cassettes.

Modern Music Center, P.O. Box 856, 413 N Parkerson, Crowley, Louisiana 70526; (318) 783-1601. Cajun music source.

Savoy's Music Center, P.O. Box 941, Eunice, Louisiana 70535, (318) 457-8490 or (318) 457-7389. Cajun music source.

Tango Catalogue, B-2, Juniper East, Yarmouth, ME 04096-1439. The catalogue features: The Best of Tango Video Series; Daniel & Rebecca's Instructional Video; Argentine Master Teachers on Video; Tango music and CDs; Cassettes; Tango Books and other products. A 1997 tour to Buenos Aires to explore the Tango in its home setting.

Tower Records, 1 (800) ASK TOWER.

CDS AND CASSETTES

Dance Plus, 2018 Granby Drive, Oakville, Ontario, Canada, L6H 3X9. Tel: (905) 849-4122, Fax: (905) 849-7085. Over 500 strict time ballroom CDs. New releases and music list available.

Dance Trax International, 2217 N. Woodbridge, Saginaw, MI 48602. Ph./Fax: (517) 799-0349. Orders 1 (800) 513-2623. CDs for International style, American style, and Showcase Dancing.

Ewers and Mine Software. 3702 SW Court Ave. Ankeny, Iowa 50021. CD Rom multi-media interactive dance instruction.

Lane, Christy. Complete Party Dance Music on CD. National Dance Association. Attention: Millie Puccio. 1900 Association Drive, Peston, Va. 20191-1598

Living Traditions, 2442 NW Market St. #168, Seattle, WA 98107. (206) 781-2238 or 1 (800) 500-2364. *Roll Up the Rug,* Triple Swing, Volume I and II and Rhythm and Blues. *Really Swingin',* Frankie Mannings, "Big-Band Favorites." *Cascade of Tears,* 15 Romantic Dances. Popular Vintage Dances, Cajun, and Zydeco music.

Musical Services, 409 Lyman Ave. Baltimore, MD 21212. Ph: (800) 892-0204, Fax: (410) 433-7948. Helmut Licht-Variety of cassettes and CDs of ballroom favorites.

Pro Dance, Suite 201, 1152 Victoria St. Lemoyne, QC, J4R 1R1, Canada. CDs for class practice or home use all in International dance rhythm (BPM).

VIDEOS

Allons Danser! Randy Speyrer, P.O. Box 15908, New Orleans, LA 70175-5908; (504) 899-0615. "Cajun Dancing" step-by-step instruction. Waltz, Two-Step, One-Step, Cajun Jitterbug.

B & M Dance Productions (AD). 6804 Newbold, Bethesda, MD 20817. American Social Dance instructional videos for beginners to advanced. "How To" tapes teach beginners to advanced steps.

Brentwood House Video, 5740 Corsa Ave., Suite 102, Westlake Village, CA 91362. "Line Dancing," "New Line Dancing," "Fun and Funky Freestyle Dancing," "Line Dancing Vol. 2," Christy Lane.

Best Film and Video Corp., Great Neck, NY 11021. "Fred Astaire Dancing: Ballroom (Foxtrot, Waltz), Latin (Cha Cha, Salsa)."

Coffey Video Productions. 3300 Gilbert Lane, Knoxville, TN 37920; (800) 423-1417. "Texas Two Step."

Dancing Times Limited, 45-47 Clerkenwell Green, London, EC1R OEB. Extensive stock of ballroom Dancing Times Books and videos.

Dance Lovers. P.O. Box 7071, Ashville, NC 28802. VHS videos, music, and tapes.

Hoctor Products for Education. P.O. Box 38, Waldwick, NJ 07463; (201) 652-7767; Fax: (201) 652-2500. "Hip Hop," "Charleston."

Human Kinetics, P.O. Box 5076, Champaign, IL 61825-5076. Social Dance Music Set, Item MGAR0191. Individual tapes cover Swing, Waltz, Cha Cha, Foxtrot, and Polka music.

Lane, Christy. Complete Guide to Party Dances. New video of most requested party dances. Electric Slide, YMCA, Macarena, Chicken Dance, Stroll, Conga, Hand JIve, Swing, ect. National Dance Association. Attention: Millie Puccio, 1900 Association Drive, Peston, Va. 20191-1598.

Let's Do It Productions, P.O. Box 5483, Spokane, WA 99205. (509) 235-6555; Fax: (509) 235-4445. Line Dance, Country Western videos and manuals.

National Association of Country Dances, P.O. Box 9841, Colorado Springs, CO 80932. "28 Country Swing Moves and Combinations."

Not Strictly Ballroom. The first complete Social Dance Library of Videotapes. Vance Productions ℅ Colortech Video Productions, 4501 College Blvd, Ste 110, Shawnee Mission, Kansas 66211-9989. Beginning, Intermediate and Advanced Series: Covers: Foxtrot, Waltz, Tango, Viennese Waltz, Rumba, Cha Cha, East Coast Swing, Samba, Mambo, Merengue, West Coast Swing, Country Western Dances: Two-Step, Waltz, Polka, Cha Cha, Eastern Swing, Western Swing, Country Line dances, the "B.C." (8 tapes in all).

PPI Parade Video, 88 St. Fancis St., Newark, NJ 17105. "Texas Dance Styles" by Valerie Moss and Scott Schmitz; "Texas Two-Step," "Down and Dirty" (Jerk, Twist, Stroll, Monkey, Hustle, etc.).

Princeton Book Co. 12 West Delaware Avenue, Pennington, NJ 08534. "Arthur Murray Dance Magic Series." Waltz, Tango, Swing, Samba, Merengue, Night Club, Rumba, Salsa, Cha Cha, Dancin' Dirty, Foxtrot, Mambo. 1 (800) 220-7149, Fax: (609) 737-1869. (30 minute tape).

———. Jitterbug: Beginners (Webb, Kyle and Susan Parisi). East Coast Swing, West Coast Swing. (60 minutes).

———. Jitterbug: Intermediate (Webb, Kyle and Susan Parisi). More stylish moves, East and West Coast Swing. (60 minutes).

———. "Sex and Social Dance." Social dance history, clips of Astaire and Rogers, rock and roll, Elvis, twist, disco scenes. (Box of 8 tapes, 60 minutes each).

Quality Video Inc., 7399 Bush Lake Road, Minneapolis, MN 55439. "Country Line Dancing for Kids," "Country Line Dancing," "More Country Line Dancing," Diane Horner.

R & R Video International Dancing in America Series. 3649 Whitter Blvd. Los Angeles, CA 90023. "West Coast Swing," Skippy Blair.

Savoy-style *Lindy Hop,* Levels 1, 2, 3. Instructional video. ***Living Traditions,*** (206) 781-2238 or 1 (800) 500-2364.

Speyrer, Cynthia and Rand Speyrer. ***Introduction to Cajun Dancing,*** Volumes I and II (video). Gretna, LA: Pelican Publishing Co., 1993.

Shim Sham (instructional video) Swing, etc., from 1930s and 1940s. ***Living Traditions,*** (206) 781-1238 or 1 (800) 500-2364.

Supreme Audio, Inc. P.O. Box 50, Marlborough, NH 03455; (800) 445-7398; Fax: (603) 876-4001. Large collection of Square, Clogging, Country Western, Texas, East Coast Swing, and West Coast Swing videos.

Tanguero Productions, 5351 Corteen Place, code ADL1, North Hollywood, CA 91607. Alberto Toledano and Loreen Arbus "Tango-Argentine Style" instructional video.

Bibliography

Ancelet, Barry Jean. *Cajun Music: Its Origins and Development.* Lafayette, Louisiana: University of Southwest Louisiana, 1989.

Bottomer, Paul. *Line Dancing.* New York, N.Y. Anness Publishers, 1996.

Bottner, Paul. *Dance Crazy Series.* Quick step, Waltz, American Line, Rock 'n' Roll, Salsa. Lorenz Books, New York, NY, 10011. (800)354-9657.

Boven, John. *South to Louisiana,* (The music of the Cajun bayous). Gretna, Louisiana: Pelican Publishing Co., 1992.

Boyd, Neville. *New Vogue Sequence Dancing.* North Star Publishers, 1989.

Collier, Simon, Artenis Cooper, Maria Susana Azzi, and Richard Martin. *Tango, The Dance, The Song, The Story.* London: Thames & Hudson Ltd., 1995.

Conrad, Glenn R. *The Cajuns: Essays on their History and Culture.* Lafayette, Louisiana: University of Southwest Louisiana, 1983.

Duke, Jerry. *Social and Ballroom Dance Lab Manual,* San Francisco, CA: Duke Publishing Co., 1988.

——. *Dance of the Cajuns.* San Francisco, CA: Duke Publishing Co., 1987.

Elfman, Bradley. *Breakdancing.* New York: Avon Books, 1984.

Evanchuk, Robin. "Cajun Sight, Sound and Movement." *Ethnic and Recreational Dance: Focus on Dance VI.* Dance Division of the American Association for Health, Physical Education and Recreation, Washington, D.C. 1972, pp. 43–46.

Fischer-Munstermann, Uta. *Jazz Dance and Jazz Gymnastics Including Disco Dancing.* New York: Sterling Publishing Co., Inc., 1978.

Fry, Macon and Julie Posner. *Cajun Country Guide.* Gretna, Louisiana: Pelican Publishing Co., 1992.

Gould, Philip. *Cajun Music and Zydeco.* Baton Rouge, Louisiana: Louisiana State University Press, 1992.

Gwynne, Michael. *Sequence Dancing.* London: A & C Black Publishers, 1985.

Hager, Steven. *Hip Hop: The Illustrated History of Break Dancing, Rap Music, and Graffiti.* New York: St. Martin's Press, 1984.

Hampshire, Harry Smith and Doreen Casey. *The Viennese Waltz.* Brooklyn, N.Y.: Revisionist Press, 1993.

Heaton, Alma and Israel Heaton. *Ballroom Dance Rhythms.* Dubuque. IA: William C. Brown Co., 1961.

Heaton, Alma. *Disco with Donny and Marie, Step by Step Guide to Disco Dancing.* CA and MT: Osmond Publishing Co., Provo, UT. 1979.

——. *Techniques or Teaching Ballroom Dance.* Provo, UT: Brigham Young University Press, 1965.

——. *Techniques of Teaching Ballroom Rhythms.* Dubuque, IA: Kendall-Hunt Publishing Co., 1971.

——. *Fun Dance Rhythms.* Provo, UT: Brigham Young University Press, 1976.

Javna, John. *How to Jitterbug.* New York: St. Martin's Press, 1984.

Kilbride, Ann and Angelo Algoso. *The Complete Book on Disco and Ballroom Dancing.* Los Alamitos, CA: Hwong Publishing Co., 1979.

Kraus, Richard. "Dance in the Age of Aquarius," *Focus on Dance VI.* Jane Harris Ericson, ed. Washington, D.C.: American Association for Health, Physical Education and Recreation, 1972, pp. 56–58.

Lane, Christy. *Complete Book of Line Dancing.* Champaign, IL., Human Kinetics, 1995.

Laird, Walter. *Technique of Latin Dancing: International Dance.* London: Book Service. New edition 1988. Reprint 1992.

——. *The Ballroom Dance Pack.* London: Dorling Kindersley. Publisher: Houghton Mifflin Co., 1994.

Livingston, Peter. *The Complete Book of Country Swing and Western Dance and a Bit About Cowboys.* Garden City, NY: Doubleday & Co., Inc., 1981.

Lustgarden, Karen. *The Complete Guide to Disco Dancing.* New York: Warner Books Inc., 1978.

Marlow, Cuirtis. *Break Dancing.* Cresskill, N.J.: Sharon Publications Inc., 1984.

Monte, John. *The Fred Astaire Dance Book.* New York: Simon and Schuster, 1978.

Moore, Alex. *Ballroom Dancing: with 100 Diagrams and Photographs of the Quickstep, Waltz, Foxtrot, Tango.* London: A & C Clark Publisher, 1986.

National Association of Country Dancers. *Country and Western Dance Manual.* P.O. Box 9841, Colorado Springs, CO. 80932.

Osborne, Hilton. *Line Dancing: Run to the Floor for Country Western.* Glendale, CA: Griffin Publisher, 1994.

Plater, Ormonde, Cynthia Speyrer and Rand Speyrer. *Cajun Dancing.* Gretna, Louisiana: Pelican Publishing Co., 1993.

Ray, Ollie Mae. *Encyclopedia of Line Dances.* Reston, Virginia 22091. National Dance Association, American Alliance for Health, Physical Education, Recreation and Dance, 1992.

Rushing Productions. 5149 Blanco Rd., #214, San Antonio, TX 78216. *"Kicker Dancin' Texas Style."* How to do the top ten Country and Western Dances like a Texas cowboy, 1982.

Sarver, Mary J. 1224 SW Normandy Terrace, Seattle, WA 98166. *"Pattern Ballroom Dances for Seniors,"* 27 dances, 1992.

Schild, Myrna Martin. SIU Box 1126, Edwardsville, IL 62026. *"Smooth Dances"* (Foxtrot, Waltz, Tango), *"Rhythm Dances"* (Polka and Regional Dances, Samba, Merengue, Swing, Mambo, Cha Cha and Rumba).

Selmon, Simon. *Let's Lindy.* U.K.: Princeton Book Co., 12 West Delaware Avenue, Pennington, NJ 08534, 1993.

Silvester, Victor. *Modern Ballroom Dancing: The Maestro's Manual,* London: Trafalgar Square Publisher, 1993.

Stephenson, Richard M. and Joseph Iaccarino. *The Complete Book of Ballroom Dancing.* New York: Doubleday, 1980.

Supreme Audio, Inc., P.O. Box 50, Marlborough, NH 03455-0050. Exclusive source for dance and fitness audio equipment. Wireless microphone systems, wireless remote wristwatches and variable speed tape deck and CD players.

Theriot, Marie del Norte and Catherine Blanchet. *Les Danses Rondes: Louisiana French Folk Dances.* Abbeville, Louisiana: R. E. Blanchet, distributor, 1955.

Thorpe, Edward. *Black Dance.* New York, NY: Overlook Press, 1989, reprint 1994.

Veloz and Yolands. *Tango and Rumba.* New York: Harper and Brothers, 1939.

Wainwright, Lyndon B. *First Steps to Ballroom Dancing.* 66 B The Broadway, Mill Hill, London N W 7 3TF, England: Lyric Books Limited, 1993.

Wilson, Charles Regan and William Ferris. *Encyclopedia of Southern Culture.* Chapel Hill, NC: University of North Carolina Press, 1989. (See entries for "Cajun Music" and "Zydeco.")

Wright, Judy Patterson. *Social Dance Steps to Success.* Leisure Press a division of Human Kinetics, P.O. Box 5076, Champaign, IL. 61825-5076.

Glossary

Accent The stress that is placed on a beat that makes it stronger or louder than the others. The primary accent is on the first beat of the measure. Sometimes there is more than one accent per measure. Some dance steps have the accent on the off-beat, which makes the rhythm syncopated.

Anchor Step West Coast Swing term. Step right behind left (hook) (count 1), step left in place (count *and*), step right in place (count 2). Usually danced at the end of the slot.

Balance *2/4 Time.* 1. Step left (count 1); touch right to left, rising on balls of both feet (count *and*); lower heels (count 2); and hold (count *and*). Repeat, beginning right. 2. Or step left (count 1) and touch right to left (count 2). Repeat same movement, beginning right. Omit the pronounced lift of the heel in this analysis. However, there should be a slight lift of the body as the movement is executed.

Banjo Position *See* Right Parallel Position.

Bossa Nova A Social Dance from Brazil.

Butterfly Position Couple faces, arms extended shoulder high and out to the sides, hands joined. In this position, couple may dance forward and backward or to the right or left, and in the line of direction and reverse line of direction.

Buzz Step A turning step used in Folk, Square, and Social Dance. Done alone or with a partner, turning clockwise or counterclockwise in swing or shoulder-waist position. Buzz step may be used to travel sideways. The rhythm is uneven (long, short). 1. *Clockwise turn.* Step right (turn toe right), pivoting clockwise on ball of foot (long); push with ball of left foot placed slightly to side of right (short). Repeat as required. Reverse footwork for counterclockwise turn. **Note:** The weight remains on the right or pivot foot; the impetus for turn is given by left foot. 2. *Sideways.* Step left sideways (long); push with right foot as it moves to the left, displacing left foot (short). **Note:** The turning action of the pivot foot is omitted.

Canter Rhythm An uneven pattern in 3/4 time, resulting from a long beat (counts 1–2) followed by a short beat (count 3). A step is taken on count 1 and held over on count 2. Another step is taken on count 3. The three-step turn in canter rhythm is step left (count 1); pivot on left a half-turn counterclockwise (count 2); step right (count 3), pivoting almost a half-turn counterclockwise; step left (count 1), completing the turn; and hold (counts 2–3). Close right to left (count 3), but keep weight on left. It may be done clockwise by starting with the right foot.

Centrifugal Force The force exerted outward from the center that is created by dancers rotating as in a buzz step swing or pivot turn.

Cha Cha Cha A Social Dance from Cuba.

Challenge Position A term used in Social Dance to refer to position of man facing woman, at approximately arm distance. Hands are not joined.

Charleston Step A step in 4/4 meter, accent on count *and.* Put weight on right bent knee, left foot in the air. Flip left foot up behind (count *and*); step forward left (count 1); bend left knee and flip right foot up behind (count *and*). Point right toe forward; straighten knees (count 2); bend left knee and flip right foot up behind (count *and*). Step back on right (count 3); bend right knee and flip left foot up behind (count *and*); point left toe behind and straighten knees (count 4).

Chassé A series of sliding steps; one foot displaces the leading one, moving forward, backward, or sideward. In Square Dance, called sashay.

Chug Step Move forward or backward on one or two feet or sideward on one foot. Moving backward on left foot, with weight on left foot and right foot slightly off the floor and knee flexed, the left foot pulls (drags) backward as the left knee straightens (count *and* 1). Body bends forward slightly with action.

Clockwise Refers to the movement of dancers around a circle in the same direction as the hands of a clock move or to a turning action of one dancer or couple as they progress around the floor. In directional terms, clockwise is to the left (e.g., "circle to the left").

Close Free foot is moved to supporting foot. Weight ends on free foot. Begin weight on left, move right (free foot) to left, and take weight on right.

Closed Position Partners stand facing each other, shoulders parallel and toes pointed directly forward. Man's right arm is around the woman and the hand is placed on the small of her back. Woman's left hand and arm rest on man's upper arm and shoulder.

Coaster Step Step back, close right to left, step forward left. Note: An option on counts 5, 6 in Sugar Push.

Conversation Position As described for open position, but with the forward hand released and arm (man's left, woman's right) hanging at the side.

Corté Social and Round dance term. *See Dip.*

Counterclockwise Refers to the movement of dancers around a circle in opposite direction from the movement of the hands on a clock or to a turning action of one dancer or couple as they progress around the floor. In directional terms, counterclockwise is to the right (e.g., "circle to the right").

Couple A man and a woman. Woman stands at man's right.

Couple Position Partners stand side by side, woman on man's right, inside hands joined, both facing in same direction. Also referred to as strolling, side-by-side, open position, or inside hands joined.

Cross-Over Position Social Dance term for Cha Cha Cha. The couple is side by side, with inside hands joined. *See* Couple Position.

Cut Time A rhythm that comes from 4/4 time. Refer to diagram on p. 12.

Dance Walk A Social Dance term that describes the basic walking step. May move forward, backward, or sideward in Foxtrot, Waltz, or Tango.

Dig Step Place slight weight on the ball of one foot; usually followed by stepping on the foot.

Dip (Corté) Step back on foot indicated, taking full weight and bending the knee. The other leg remains extended at the knee and ankle, forming a straight line from the hip. The toe remains in contact with the floor.

Disco Dance A descriptive term that encompasses a wide variety of dance steps to many rhythms of recorded music. (*See* Disco Dance, pp. 33–52).

Discotheque A French word meaning "a place where records (disques) are stored." In common usage, it describes a place for contemporary dancing to records as opposed to live music.

Draw Step In 2/4 time, step sideward on left (count 1) and draw right to left, transferring weight to right (count 2). To draw, the foot is dragged along the floor. In 3/4 time, step sideward on left (counts 1–2) and draw right to left (count 3).

Escort Position Couple faces line of direction, woman to man's right. The woman slips her left arm through the man's right arm, which is bent at the elbow so that her left hand may rest on his right forearm. Free arm hangs to side.

Even Rhythm When the beats in the rhythm pattern are all the same value, the rhythm is said to be even.

Facing Position *See* Two Hands Joined Position.

Fan A term used to describe a manner of executing a leg motion, in which the free leg swings in a whip-like movement around a small pivoting base. Should be a small, subtle action initiated in the hip.

First Position One of five basic positions of the feet used in classical ballet. The heels remain touching as the feet are rotated 180° to form one line.

Flare An exaggerated lift of the foot from the floor accompanying a knee bend. It is often used in the Tango.

Flirtation Position Partners are facing; man's left hand and woman's right hand are joined. The arms are bent and are firm so as to indicate or receive a lead.

Four Wall Dances. *See* p.88

Foxtrot An American Social Dance.

Grapevine Step left to side (count 1), step right behind left (count 2), step left to side (count 3) and step right in front of left (count 4). Bend knees, let hips turn naturally, and keep weight on balls of feet.

Hesitation A Social Dance step that cues step hold, step hold.

Hitch A Country Western Dance term. Swing right (left) knee almost waist height as one step hops on the other foot, slight chug back. Step hop is subtle.

Jitterbug An American Social Dance done to jazz or swing music. *See* Lindy.

Jody Position *See* Varsouvienne Position.

Left Parallel Position *See* Parallel Position.

Lindy An American Social Dance done to jazz or swing music in 4/4 or cut time. There are three Lindy rhythms–single, double, and triple.

Line A type of formation. Dancers stand side by side, all facing in the same direction.

Magic Step A Social Dance term. A basic step of the American Foxtrot.

Measure One measure encloses a group of beats made by the regular occurrence of the heavy accent. It represents the underlying beat enclosed between two adjacent bars on a musical staff.

Meter Refers to time in music or group of beats to form the underlying rhythms within a measure.

Note Values A term used to refer to the relative value of the musical notes or beats that make up the rhythmic pattern.

Open Position Partners stand side by side, woman on man's right, facing in the same direction. Man's right arm is around woman's waist. Woman's left hand rests on man's right shoulder. Man holds woman's right hand in his left. Arms extend easily forward.

Parallel Position Refers to right or left parallel position. Right parallel is a variation of closed position, in which both man and woman are turned one-eighth turn counterclockwise to a position facing diagonal. The woman is slightly in front of but to the right of the man. Also referred to as banjo position. In left parallel position, man and woman are turned clockwise to face diagonally on the other side. Woman is in front of and to the left of the man.

Partner Woman to immediate *right* of man and man to immediate *left* of woman.

Phrase A musical term that represents a short division of time comprising a complete thought or statement. In dance, it is a series of movements considered as a unit in a dance pattern. It is a group of measures, generally four or eight, but sometimes 16 to 32.

Pivot Turn clockwise or counterclockwise on balls of one or both feet.

Pivot Turn Closed or shoulder-waist position. Step left, pivoting clockwise (count 1), continuing in same direction step right (count 2); step left (count 3), and step right (count 4). Make one complete turn progressing in line of direction. May also be done counterclockwise. Refer to p. 31.

Pivot Turn Dip Step left, turn clockwise (count 1); step back on right, continuing turn (count 2); step left, facing forward (count 3); dip back on right foot, still facing forward (count 4).

Pressure Lead A lead in which extra pressure is exerted by the fingers, arm, or body in order to lead the woman into a particular position or step.

Push Step Moving to the left, beginning left, step (chug) to the side (count 1); bring right toe close to left instep; and push right foot away from body (count *and*). Repeat pattern. The push step is similar to a buzz step, except that the action is taken to the side instead of in a turning or circling movement.

Q Symbol for Quick. Used for Rhythm Cue. For example, QQSS, Quick Quick Slow Slow.

Quick A rhythm cue. For example, 4/4 time, 4 quarter beats to each measure; each beat is given the same amount of time, an accent on the first beats of the measure. When a step is taken on each beat (1-2-3-4), these are called *quick* beats. When steps are taken only on 1 and 3, they are twice as long and are called *slow* beats.

Reverse Open Position From an open Social Dance position, facing line of direction, partners turn in toward each other to face reverse line of direction but do not change arm or hand positions.

Reverse Varsouvienne position Couples are standing almost side by side, with the woman on the left side of the man. She is slightly behind him. The man reaches across in front of the woman to hold her left hand in his left. Her right arm is around his shoulders and her right hand grasps his right hand at shoulder level. For Social Dance, the right arm is sometimes extended behind partner at waist level and grasps his hand at the waist. Still a different concept of reverse Varsouvienne position is merely to turn half about from Varsouvienne position. Now the woman is on man's left side but slightly in front of him, and his left arm is around her shoulders. Her right arm is across in front of him.

Rhythm Pattern The rhythm pattern in dance is the grouping of beats for the pattern of a dance step. The rhythm pattern must correspond to the underlying beat of the music.

Right Parallel Position *See* Parallel Position.

Rock A dance term used when the dancer steps forward (or backward) a short step and then backward (or forward) a short step. With the body weight shifting forward and backward over the foot, this creates a rocking motion. The term is used in Social Dance and in American Round Dance and Folk Dance.

Rock-and-Roll When the second and fourth beats are accented in country-western and folk blues music, it is referred to as rock-and-roll music. Contemporary fad dances are done to rock-and-roll music. Rock-and-roll is a rhythm; but the term *Rock Dance* is used.

Rumba A Latin-American Dance from Cuba in 4/4 time.

Samba A Latin-American Dance from Brazil in 4/4 or cut time.

Scoot A Country Western Dance term. *See* Chug Step.

Scuff A Country Western Dance term. A brush of the heel forward.

Semiopen Position A Social Dance position halfway between open and closed position.

Shine Position A social dance term. The man faces the woman at approximately arms distance. Hands are not joined. Also called the Challenge Position.

Sidecar Position *See* Left Parallel Position; Parallel Position.

Side Step Step to the left with the left foot (count 1). Close right to left, take weight on right (count 2).

Skip A basic form of locomotion in uneven rhythm. The pattern is a step and a hop on the same foot in slow quick slow quick rhythm.

Slot Dance The West Coast Swing is referred to as a slot dance because couples move forward and backward in a narrow space.

Slow A rhythm cue. *See* Quick.

Stamp Place the ball of one foot firmly on the floor, accenting the placement. The weight is not usually transferred to the foot taking the stamp; however, in some instances, it does take the weight.

Step Close Step sideward left (count 1), and close right to left, take weight on right (count 2). The right foot does not draw along the floor, but moves freely into place beside left.

Step-Hop Step on the left foot (count 1) and hop on the same foot (count *and*). Even rhythm.

Step Swing Step left (count 1) and swing right across in front of left (count 2). Repeat movement, beginning right.

Stride Position A Social Dance term. Legs straight, feet apart.

Strut Walk forward, upper torso high and leading, left knee slightly bent, toe pointed, preparing to step. Step on *ball of foot first* and then lower heel gently.

Suzy Q Moving sideward, toes are together, heels apart, "pigeon toes." Weight on both feet, shift weight to left heel, right toe simultaneously, pivoting to "pigeon toe" position; shift weight to left toe, right heel, pivoting to toes out, "roach toe." Alternating toe heel, heel toe, move sideward.

Sweep Cue word for Varsouvienne and Country Western Line Dances as left heel swings across in front of right instep. Same as wing.

Sweetheart Position Country Western dance position. Same as the Varsouvienne position.

Swing Out Position *See* Flirtation Position.

Swivel Toes and heels move sideward, either weight on toes, pivoting heels, or weight on heels, pivoting toes. Also called Suzy Q. Or, pivoting on one toe and one heel simultaneously, then pivoting on the other toe and heel, alternating toe heel, heel toe, moving sideward; or, in place by shifting weight, feet are "pigeon toes," then heels together, toes pointed out "roach toe."

Swivel Turn In one spot, a complete turn on the ball of one foot, either direction. Free foot may be lifted, bending knee, or close to other heel.

Syncopation A temporary displacement of the natural accent in music. For instance, shifting the accent from the naturally strong first and third beat to the weak second and fourth beat.

Tango A Latin American Dance from Argentina.

Tempo Rate of speed at which the music is played, or the speed of the dance.

Time Signature A symbol indicating duration of time. Example: In 2/4 time, the upper number indicates number of beats per measure, while the lower number indicates the note value that receives one beat.

Twinkle Step A variation based on box rhythms for both Foxtrot and Waltz.

Two Hands Joined Position Partners stand facing each other, shoulders parallel, and toes pointed directly forward. Two hands are joined, man's palms up, his thumbs on top of her hands. The elbows are bent and held close to the body.

Two–Step Step left (count 1), close right to left (count 2), step left (count 3), and hold (count 4).

Uneven Rhythm When the beats in the rhythm pattern are not all the same value but are a combination of slow and quick beats, the rhythm is said to be uneven.

Varsouvienne Position Couple faces in line of direction, woman in front and slightly to the right of man. Man holds woman's left hand in his left at shoulder level. Man's right arm extends back of woman's shoulders and holds woman's raised right hand in his right. In Social Dance, this is sometimes called jody position.

Walk A basic form of locomotion in even rhythm. Steps are from one foot to the other, the weight being transferred from heel to toe.

Waltz Step forward left (count 1), step sideward right (count 2), close left to right, and take weight left (count 3).

Waltz Balance *See* Balance, 3/4 time.

Wrap Position The woman is at the right of the man. His right arm is around her waist and his hand holds her left hand. His left hand is holding her right hand in front.

Dance Index

Subject Index